12/11

HELPING HOUNDS
THE STORY OF ASSISTANCE DOGS

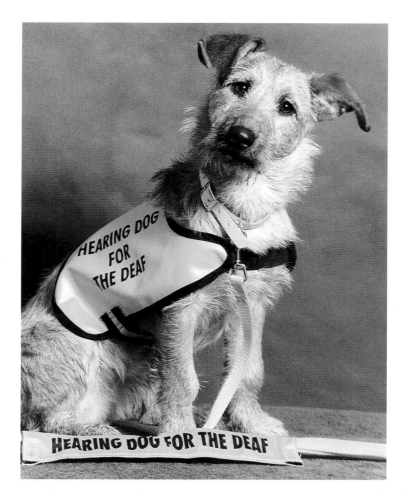

Alison Hornsby

RINGPRESS

Published by Ringpress Books Limited,
PO Box 8, Lydney, Gloucestershire,
GL15 4YN, United Kingdom.

First published 2000
©2000 Ringpress Books Limited. All rights reserved

ISBN 1 86054 157 7

Printed and bound in Hong Kong by Printworks International Ltd.

Photos courtesy of Sheila Atter, Guide Dogs for the Blind Association, Dogs for the Disabled,
Hearing Dogs for Deaf People, and Pets as Therapy, unless otherwise credited.

INTRODUCTION

Owning a dog gives people all over the world great pleasure and companionship, but it is easy to forget that many of them do a job beyond that of loyal companion. As the traditional canine 'jobs' are on the decline – dogs as herders, drovers, ratters etc. – another area is on the increase: that of assistance dogs.

Dogs have the ability and willingness to help disabled people enjoy a better quality of life. They do this in many ways:

• As Guide Dogs for the Blind, enabling the visually impaired to travel independently and safely in today's increasingly difficult environment.
• As Dogs for the Disabled, helping their owners with tasks that most of us find easy and yet mean the difference between dependence and independence to disabled people.
• As Hearing Dogs for Deaf People, providing a communication link with the hearing world that technology cannot imitate.
• As Therapy Dogs, giving friendship and affection.

In addition to their assistance, these dogs provide companionship which is invaluable to those who live alone. They reduce stress and feelings of isolation, and have been shown to have clear and measurable effects on the feelings of wellbeing in humans.

For the first time ever, the work of assistance dog charities has been examined in depth, looking at the intensive training that goes into producing these remarkable dogs. From planning breeding programmes, through to the dogs' retirement, this book follows the training process every step of the way.

Recipients talk about their own experiences, too, and the incredibly close relationships they build with their companions and aids. An assistance dog is so much more than an aid to pick up a dropped sock or to alert his owner to the ringing telephone. As well as providing practical help, the case histories show how dogs have given their owners a renewed sense of confidence and independence, and enabled them to create entirely new and fulfilling lives for themselves.

The heart-warming tales of human/dog relationships are evidence that all the money and hard work that goes into training assistance dogs are very worthwhile investments. Enhancing their owners' lives, and giving them love and support, these dogs truly are man's best friend.

1 GUIDE DOGS

Training a Guide Dog is one of the most complex and difficult tasks in the field of dog training. Other working dogs rely on natural and instinctive behaviour – sight, smell, hearing and pack animal behaviour. The Guide Dog, by contrast, has to perform his task while suppressing these inherited instincts. When working, he must not chase, use his nose, or be distracted. He must concentrate on the job in hand to the exclusion of all distractions – other than those around which he must guide his owner.

The role of a dog leading a blind person is not a new one. The Metropolitan Museum in New York has a Chinese scroll dating from the 13th century, showing a blind man being led by a dog. Similar scenes have been depicted in woodcuts, paintings and engravings from the 16th century. Gainsborough (1727-1788) shows a dog leading its master in his painting *Blind Man on a Bridge*. But it was not until after the First World War that formal techniques were used to train what we now refer to as Guide Dogs for the Blind.

HISTORY OF THE GUIDE DOG

The Guide Dog movement started in Germany. The German Red Cross Ambulance Dogs Association trained dogs to help find the

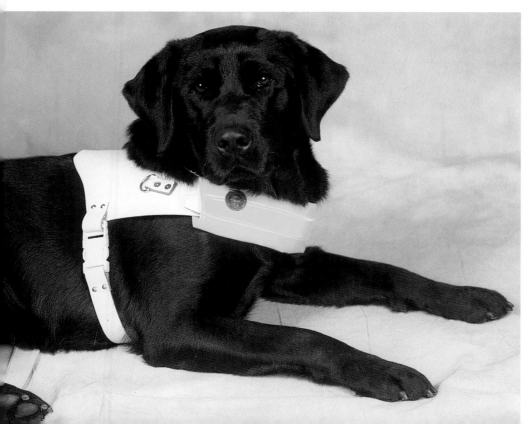

Training a Guide Dog involves considerable specialist training, but the rewards for the eventual owner are immeasurable.

A trainer wearing blindfold goggles. A similar method is still used today in the latter stages of training.

In the early days of the Guide Dog movement, German Shepherds were the standard dogs used.

wounded on battlefields. Seeing their potential for other uses, the Association started training dogs to lead veterans who were blinded during the First World War. By 1919, more than 500 war-blinded men had been provided with Guide Dogs, many of which were German Shepherds.

By the mid-1920s, the popularity of the German Shepherd had spread enormously. The German Red Cross had difficulties acquiring enough suitable dogs, so the German Ministry of Labour asked the German Shepherd Dog Association to provide suitable Guide Dogs. A large new training school at Potsdam was opened in 1923, rapid progress was made and, by the early 1930s, they had trained more than 4,000 German Shepherds as Guide Dogs.

The controller of this training school identified three key factors to producing successful Guide Dogs:
1) The selection of good-quality dogs, physically sound and of good temperament.

2) Matching the dog's ability to the owner's ability and requirements.
3) Continued support once the dog and owner have returned home after training.
These fundamental principles have not changed.

The reputation of the work being carried out at the Potsdam school spread worldwide. In 1927, Dorothy Eustis, an American lady living in Switzerland, visited the centre. She went on to be largely responsible for initiating the guide dog movement in America and Great Britain. At her kennels, known as Fortunate Fields, Dorothy was breeding and training German Shepherds for the army, police and customs services. The principal purpose of Fortunate Fields was to develop a selective breeding programme that would produce dogs suitable for a wide range of work. This later included careful selection of stock suitable for Guide Dog work.

In 1928, Dorothy trained her first two German Shepherd Guide Dogs. An enthusiastic young

The first four Guide Dogs to be trained in Britain, October 1931.

American, Morris Frank, persuaded her to provide him with one of these dogs. Together with his new dog, Buddy, Morris returned to the United States. Shortly afterwards, Dorothy Eustis also returned to her native country and, in partnership with Morris Frank, set about the daunting task of launching 'The Seeing Eye' organisation.

By 1931, Dorothy Eustis was in a position to send William Debetaz, an instructor from The Seeing Eye school in America, to train the first four British Guide Dogs and their owners. They were all German Shepherds.

In the 1930s, when The Guide Dogs for the Blind Association relied on adult dogs donated by the public, German Shepherds and Border Collies were the most common breeds offered. Due to the popularity of the German Shepherd in the 1920s, many people were prepared to pay high prices for the breed and this inevitably encouraged a great deal of indiscriminate breeding, resulting in many shy, nervous specimens.

With the outbreak of the Second World War, pedigree dog breeding declined, resulting in fewer good-quality German Shepherds being offered to the Association. Attention was turned to other breeds. A variety were tried – Border Collies, Dalmatians, Airedales and all types of retriever – but, at that time, only the Border Collie was judged to have the qualities needed

After the war, German Shepherds reappeared as Guide Dogs in greater numbers. It was some time before the quality of the Labrador improved enough to be considered suitable for regular use – which seems surprising, as the breed now dominates the Guide Dog population the world over.

With the variety of types being offered at the time, the wastage rate was high. Finding healthy dogs with a confident attitude was difficult. For more than 30 years, the Association obtained dogs from various sources: farmers, dealers and breeders. These dogs were neither bred nor reared for this highly specialised and demanding work. A puppy-rearing scheme was introduced in the mid-1950s, as it was recognised that prospective guide dogs needed special treatment as puppies. This

Alfred Morgan and Bella, who were on the second Guide Dog class in Britain in October 1932.

was followed by a small breeding programme.

By the end of 1961, the Association owned two German Shepherd and five Labrador brood bitches. The qualities of the Labrador proved a more suitable match for the increasing diversity of applicants applying for Guide Dogs. The breeding programme had to develop to produce a wide range of dog, both in size and temperament. Tall people need a large dog, and the elderly or physically less capable require a more sensitive temperament that is easy to handle.

Today, the majority of dogs trained as Guide Dogs in the UK are bred by the Guide Dogs for the Blind Association.

CASE HISTORY

LISA POTTER AND JESSIE

Name: Lisa Potter.
Guide Dog: Jessie, a Labrador.
Family: New baby.
Occupation/interests: Maternity leave from job as an admissions information assistant at a university.

Lisa's graduation day. After years of accompanying Lisa to lectures, it was natural that Jessie should be there too.

My eye-sight problem was initially overlooked, and I was dismissed merely as a clumsy child. After a private consultation with yet another ophthalmologist, astigmatism was diagnosed, which, I was told, could be corrected with the use of glasses.

"As I got older, it was obvious that glasses were not helping. Further tests, when I was 11 years old, revealed I had tunnel vision, caused by retinitis pigmentosa. While in hospital, I had terrible stomach pains, and tests revealed proteins in my urine. They eventually found me to have polycystic kidney disease, which was connected to my eye condition and together it is called 'Senior syndrome'.

"My mum and dad applied to puppy-walk for the Guide Dogs for the Blind Association. At present, they are puppy-walking their 15th puppy, 12 of which have qualified as Guide Dogs and one is still in training. On one of the many open days at our nearest training centre, I picked up a leaflet about training with a Guide Dog.

"Up until this point, I thought the vision I still had would prohibit me from having a dog. With tunnel vision, I could see enough to be able to read, as long as the print was large and clear. I was able to walk around by myself, with the use of a long cane to help increase my mobility and confidence, but I had no spatial awareness or sense of direction and would frequently walk into objects.

"I applied for a Guide Dog at the age of 18, just before I was due to start at Swansea University. The thought of finding my way around the complex was daunting and I thought a dog would give me greater independence. Unfortunately, I was turned down.

"An instructor came, interviewed and assessed me and my situation, and decided I had enough to cope with – not only was university just around the corner, but I was soon to start on home dialysis. It was recommended that I re-apply in a year's time, when I had settled into my new surroundings and the routine of regular trips home for dialysis.

"I re-applied a year later. Because I still had a small degree of useful vision, I was invited to attend a further assessment course. The first time I went out with an instructor to work with one of the trainee dogs, I knew it was for me, and just hoped that the instructor would think the same. It was the most

Jessie with Emlyn, the Guide Dog puppy that Lisa's parents are puppy-walking.

amazing feeling to walk down the road being guided by a dog. Normally, I would have been walking very slowly, concentrating on looking at the ground and trying hard to avoid people and lampposts. Instead, I was able to walk with my head up, confidently enjoying the walk. I thought: 'I could definitely get use to this!' At the end of the short course, I was told that I had passed!

"Surprisingly, I didn't have to wait long to be matched to a suitable dog. Being young and active, I needed an equally bright, enthusiastic type of dog, one that could cope with my constantly changing routines at home and at university. Most importantly, I am just over five feet tall and slightly built, so wasn't able physically to handle a large, strong, boisterous dog. So yellow Labrador Jessie, at 49 lb, with a confident, willing attitude, suited me perfectly.

"I remember hearing Jessie before I met her. Sitting in my bedroom at the training centre, waiting for the dog to arrive, I heard Emma, the instructor, coming up the stairs and this frantic scrabbling sound of four feet on a slippery floor. Emma knocked and then opened the bedroom door. She made Jessie sit, took off her lead and left us to get acquainted. I called my new friend to me and Jessie got

down on her belly and crept across the carpet towards me, her tail wagging furiously. The dog rolled on to her back and started to groan. I rubbed her tummy and we had a cuddle.

"Jessie was quick to spot the rubber ring I had brought from home. She ran to get it and we were soon having a good tugging session. I threw the toy and she fetched it. She was so attentive, alert and willing to please, I felt confident that we were going to get along fine.

"I also remember being amazed at how Jessie would dive into her harness. All I had to do was hold it in front of her and she would walk in. Her tail constantly wags, and even now as an older dog she really looks as if she thoroughly enjoys her work.

"As training progressed, we started to do routes on our own. Emma would give us the directions and off we would go – unbelievably, we would arrive at the right place. At the end of the first week, I had to go home for dialysis. Jessie stayed at the training centre. It was so hard leaving her, I didn't want to go. But when I came back, Jessie was so pleased to see me, it was clear she was beginning to accept me as her new owner.

"Striding out confidently in the sunshine was a real treat. We walked through busy shopping areas and quieter back streets, travelled on the bus and train, walked in and out of lifts and went up and down steps – these were just some of the skills Jessie and I had to perfect before we could go home.

"We seemed to sail through training, not making too many mistakes. On one occasion, Jessie walked me into a bin attached to a lamppost. I struck the bin with my right shoulder, and it hurt quite a bit. I had to correct Jessie, and she looked so sorry for herself. When we went back to do that stretch of the pavement again, Jessie gave the lamppost a wide berth.

"Another incident during our training occurred when we were doing a walk not long after it had rained. We came to a right-turn kerb with a car parked close to the corner. In front of the car was a large puddle. Jessie wanted to walk me into the car rather than go

Jessie soon makes puppy-
walked pups feel at home.

through the puddle and get her feet wet! She still hates walking through puddles and will do her best to avoid them, making me walk through them instead. In fact, she hates the rain altogether.

"When we returned home, we had to practise the routes around the university. As it was still August and the summer vacation, it was quieter and we could practise in peace. At the beginning of term in October, Jessie still remembered all the routes perfectly.

"Jessie quickly got used to my weekly time-table. I think she knew better than me where I had to be and when. It took a while to get the other students to understand they should not talk to or make a fuss of Jessie while she was working. I put some posters up, explaining how important it was to ignore her, which really helped.

"My degree course included German, Italian and Business Studies. As part of the course, I had to go to Germany for a year. Unfortunately, because of the quarantine laws, I was unable to take Jessie with me and was apprehensive about going. Finding my way

around a strange place, using a long cane again, and coping with a foreign language, albeit one I was studying, were major difficulties which I had to overcome.

"I began to realise just what Jessie did for me, especially after a near miss with a tram, which really shook me up – I was concentrating so much on remembering the route, I was not paying attention to the traffic. My first thought after I recovered was: 'If only I had Jessie!'

"During my five years at university, I was dialysing three times a week, my health was deteriorating noticeably and my walking speed got slower as my energy levels decreased. Jessie was always quick to respond to this and adjust her speed accordingly. To dialyse, we had to travel home to Newport from Swansea by train. Jessie loved the train – she was quick to learn the route through to the carriage next to the buffet car, so I could get a drink on the journey. She always went to the same table and would be rather displeased if there was someone else in what she considered to be our seat.

Lisa and Jessie with a visiting Guide Dog owner from Japan.

"Dialysing is a slow, boring process. Jessie would keep me company during the long hours in the special cabin that had been erected in the garden. The only time we had to send her out was when I got leg cramps, caused by low blood pressure. Dad would have to thump my legs, causing me great pain, which would make me cry. Not understanding what was happening, Jessie would get rather worried.

"Jessie, my constant companion, also attended my graduation. We walked across the stage together; it was a proud moment. I think Jessie should have got a degree as well as me – after all, she did attend all the lectures with me!

"In 1995, I got the telephone call I had been waiting for. A kidney transplant was available and I had to go to hospital at once. I didn't see Jessie again for 16 days. I came out of hospital on my birthday and there was the best present of all – Jessie wagging her tail and groaning at me as usual.

"Once I'd fully recovered from the operation, it was time to start job hunting. The Disability Employment Office advisor wrote to several companies on my behalf, but all the applications came back with a negative response. I was beginning to wonder if having Jessie was affecting my employment opportunities.

"A few weeks later, I received a telephone call from the Disability Employment Office offering me a job as an administration assistant. I stayed for a year. The staff were great and everyone made Jessie and me so welcome. She was allowed to roam around the office and sit by whoever she chose to accompany that day. It was the perfect position for me – not only did I gain experience, but confidence as well.

"My second job was as a personal assistant to the district manager of a company in Cardiff. It was only a maternity-cover post, but gave me invaluable experience. Obviously, my previous employers were used to dealing with people with a disability, but here was something new. It took a while for the other staff members to treat me in the same way as everyone else and to realise that I was quite capable of doing the job I was employed to do. Jessie was good at breaking the ice.

"My current job is as an admissions information assistant at the University of Wales College, Newport. Here Jessie and I are very much part of the team. They don't

Jessie enjoys accompanying Lisa on boating trips – as long as she doesn't have to get her feet wet.

The meticulous breeding programme ensures only the very best Guide Dogs are produced.

employ any other disabled people, but they are used to dealing with disabled students. I don't feel that I have been discriminated against in my search for work, but the hardest part is finding someone who will give you a chance. Whatever your disability, you deserve the right to be employed.

"I'm actually on maternity leave now, and am the only kidney transplant recipient to have gone almost full-term, carrying her baby. I have a boy, born 6lb 4oz, called Dominic (meaning the gift of god). Jessie now looks upon Dominic as being another one of the family, for which she considers herself responsible.

"Having Jessie has changed my life. Since a child, I have wanted the freedom other children had, walking off by themselves as I hung on to my mother in case I lost her. I would never have contemplated going shopping in Swansea before I had my dog. I can't imagine not having her around; she has become an extension to myself.

"Jessie has given me freedom to live as normal a life as possible and to get out there and be a part of life. If anyone is ever unsure whether they should apply for a Guide Dog, I would thoroughly recommend it. They have to be prepared to cater for the daily needs of a dog. But in the end, it is worth the responsibility of looking after a dog for the extra pleasure you can get out of life. **,**

SOURCE OF GUIDE DOGS

Every year, the breeding manager purchases around a hundred puppies as prospective breeding stock. This introduces new lines to the breeding programme as part of the ongoing need to maintain or improve the quality of dog used.

Annually, some 1,100 puppies are born, which are puppy-walked as prospective Guide Dogs or future breeding stock. On average, each brood bitch will have four litters. Future breeding stock will be ear-marked from the bitch's third or fourth litter to replace the brood bitch once she has retired. The temperamental characteristics of the brood bitch are assessed so they can be matched to a suitable stud dog.

The success rate of each litter is recorded. In addition, the training department staff make comments on the qualities of the whole litter, and their strengths and weaknesses in training and matching. This enables the breeding manager to decide on which stud dog to use on each individual brood bitch when planning future matings.

The breeding programme now has more than 230 brood bitches and 60 stud dogs. All prospective breeding stock receive a thorough health-check before being retained as part of the breeding programme. Hips and elbows are X-rayed for any signs of dysplasia or osteochondrosis, and eyes are tested for any abnormalities. German Shepherds are blood-tested for haemophilia.

The demand to produce a certain number of puppies each year requires special expertise in when to mate a bitch to gain maximum numbers within a litter. Bitches are screened and swabbed during their season to ensure mating occurs on the optimum day. Stud dogs are checked twice a year to test that they are fertile. The sperm is assessed numerically and for motility. Regular monitoring has achieved a 93 per cent conception rate.

At present, the breeding centre does not carry out any artificial insemination matings, but it does store semen for probable export in the future to other Guide Dog breeding establishments. It is also a means of ensuring that successful lines can be revived in the future should the need arise.

SELECTION OF STOCK

When selecting dogs within the breeds most commonly used as Guide Dogs, there are certain breed-related factors that can either aid or hinder the training process. The following breeds are used as Guide Dogs:

LABRADOR RETRIEVER

• An easy-going, friendly, willing nature makes him generally responsive to training and control.
• Very adaptable, he can be matched to a wide range of recipients.
• Early maturity means he can come in for training earlier than most breeds and therefore has a longer working life.
• His coat is easy to care for, although some owners find Labrador hair a drawback to living with the breed.
• He has a popular image with the general public.
• Labradors have a 65 per cent success rate (1998 figures), and Labrador crosses have a 74 per cent success rate.
Some of the less favourable factors associated with the breed are his propensity to sniff and scavenge – the Labrador is always hungry! This can prove a distraction from the job in hand.

However, the positive aspects of this breed have made the Labrador so successful, that he is

The Labrador has a friendly, laid-back attitude which makes him a good Guide Dog candidate.

becoming the standard breed used in Guide Dog schools throughout the world.

GOLDEN RETRIEVER

• He has a delightfully affable gentle disposition, with a useful level of concentration and initiative.
• Less likely to scavenge than the Labrador.
• Does not shed his coat as much as the Labrador.
• Like the Labrador, the Golden Retriever has a 65 per cent success rate (1998 figures), and Golden crosses have a 74 per cent success rate.

The Golden Retriever is generally slower to mature than the Labrador. If the behaviour established in training is maintained, however, his ability will improve as he matures.

There are aspects of his temperament which can slow his progress in training – a combination of medium to high sensitivities can affect his willingness and use of initiative. ('Sensitivities' refers to the degree to which dogs are sensitive to touch, sound and their handler's tone of voice and treatment of them.) His attention-seeking

Like the Labrador, the Golden Retriever has a high success rate as a Guide Dog.

behaviour, coupled with slow maturity, can make him less easy to match.

The Golden Retriever finds changing loyalty difficult, so the transition from puppy-walker, to trainer, to Guide Dog owner in the early days of training can be a trying time for the dog and his new owner. Any concerns on the dog's part usually result in a drop in willingness, which can be difficult for some blind people to cope with and can sometimes be misinterpreted as stubbornness.

GERMAN SHEPHERD DOG

Not all blind people want a German Shepherd, or perhaps someone in the immediate family is reluctant to have one living with them. However, the German Shepherd Dog has many qualities:
- A high level of initiative
- Quick to learn.
- Capable of taking on a high workload
- An acceptable degree of concentration
- Easy gait to follow.
- Well-behaved socially and can be less distracted by other dogs than the other breeds used.

- German Shepherds have a 58 per cent success rate (1998 figures).

Early socialisation with an experienced puppy-walker is required to encourage the dog to be confident with strangers and to control the breed's natural tendency to herd and chase.

The more sensitive types are less suited to Guide Dog work. These dogs find the time spent in the kennel environment during the lengthy training programme an additional burden. Sensitive, they take longer to adapt to change, and are generally slow to mature – which all adds to their training time.

The German Shepherd Guide Dog needs a sympathetic, agile owner who can keep pace with the dog's long stride. He must also be quick-thinking and able to provide the level of work that the breed requires.

The sheer size of the German Shepherd can ensure an easier passage for the Guide Dog owner, but speed control in busy areas is an important aspect of their training. They are inclined to rush their work and enthusiastically anticipate commands if allowed. The correct

Although the German Shepherd isn't used as extensively nowadays, he still has a lot to offer as a Guide Dog.

approach from the handler is essential to develop a calm, relaxed, steady attitude in the dog. Most Guide Dog owners who have lived and worked with a German Shepherd request another one when the time comes for a replacement.

In the UK, during 1996, less than five per cent of the dogs that qualified as Guide Dogs with new owners were German Shepherds.

LABRADOR-GOLDEN RETRIEVER CROSSES

- They seem to inherit the good qualities of both breeds (see above pp14-15).
- Easy to control.
- Suitable for a wide range of owners, they are easy to match.
- As the average age of Guide Dog owners is increasing and the charity is widening the ability range of people trained, this type of dog will continue to be extremely useful.
- Labrador-Golden Retriever crosses have a 79 per cent success rate (1998 figures).

In the early seventies, the late Derek Freeman, Guide Dogs' breeding manager at that time, decided to experiment with crossing the Labrador and the Golden Retriever. The pure-bred Labrador males were rather strong and boisterous, with medium to low sensitivities. It was felt that the success rate of the males could be improved if they could increase the willingness and body sensitivity of the Labrador and lower the levels of sensitivity in the Golden Retriever. Using established pure-bred lines, the first crossbreed matings were carried out. They were an immediate success.

Derek went on to experiment with keeping first-crosses as breeding stock. The puppies produced from these matings were disappointing. High levels of body and mental sensitivity, were evident and the success rate declined. It was soon decided only to concentrate on producing first-crosses. These continue to be enormously successful.

BORDER COLLIE

- He is easy to follow, but needs the sort of owner who has a brisk walking speed and is light on his feet.

The Border Collie needs an owner with a busy lifestyle who can cope with the collie's need to be physically and mentally active.

- The breed's speed of response to commands means he needs an owner equally swift to react.
- The owner must lead a busy lifestyle to occupy the Border Collie brain.
- Statistically, the Border Collie falls into the 'miscellaneous breeds' category, which covers those breeds not included in the main stock used (i.e. Labrador Retriever, Golden Retriever, German Shepherd, Labrador crosses and Golden Retriever crosses). This miscellaneous group has just a 29 per cent success rate.

Only a small number of pure-bred Border Collies qualify each year. Training them is not difficult, but matching them to a prospective owner is.

Because it was having difficulty in establishing pure-bred lines suitable for Guide Dog work, Guide Dogs for the Blind decided to cross-breed the Border Collie with the Golden Retriever. The addition of the Retriever softens the collie drive, giving a calmer attitude, with increased confidence and less 'sound shyness'.

CURLY COATED RETRIEVER-LABRADOR CROSS

The Curly Coated Retriever is another breed that has proved more successful when crossed with the

Labrador. The phlegmatic attitude of the Curly Coated Retriever needs an injection of the Labrador's responsiveness and willingness.

- Very suitable for mature Guide Dog owners who have slow reflexes and poor balance.
- They suit the requirement usually filled by a mature Guide Dog returned for training because the owner has died or no longer requires the dog.
- Labrador crosses overall have a 74 per cent success rate (1998 figures).

THE IDEAL GUIDE DOG

Dogs are individuals with variable characteristics, so understanding and correctly assessing each dog is important. This will enable the trainer to apply the correct approach and attitude for realising the dog's full potential.

The physical criterion for a working Guide Dog required of all breeds is that they are of a minimum height, at the withers, of 19 inches. They should be of sound conformation, good stamina and have an even gait that is easy to follow. They require a coat that is both waterproof and easily managed, and they should be early maturing, with longevity, to provide as long a working life as possible.

The type of dog that is most desirable for training has temperamental qualities that affect hearing, body and mental sensitivity in the medium range. Dogs assessed to have low sensitivities are often unresponsive, with low willingness; the other extreme – high sensitivities – can produce a dog that is over-reactive, unreliable and usually unsound.

QUALITIES REQUIRED IN A GUIDE DOG
- Stable and of a pleasing disposition.
- Not neurotic, shy or frightened.
- Reasonably energetic but not hyperactive.
- Non-aggressive (not dominant, apprehensive or protective).
- A low chase instinct.
- An ability to concentrate for long periods.
- Not easily distracted.
- Willing and responsive to the human voice.
- Confident with, and tolerant of, other animals and children.

The ideal Guide Dog should be able to concentrate in all types of situation.

- Not sound-shy.
- Able to show a level of initiative.
- Not too dominant or self-interested.
- An acceptable level of body, hearing and mental sensitivity.
- As free as possible from hereditary defects.
- Ability to maintain concentration on a given task.
- Should be easily controlled, both vocally and physically, even when distracted by a sight, scent or sound within the environment.
- An adaptable attitude.

The last point is crucial. The dog must be able to cope with handler changes – from puppy-walker, to trainer, on to an instructor and finally to the Guide Dog owner.

The routine and environmental changes are enormous. The puppy starts off in the quiet relaxed environment of the home, where a routine quickly becomes established. He is then brought into the training centre kennel environment. Once qualified, he moves into the Guide Dog owner's home.

To cope with these necessary changes the dog needs to be of sound temperament and display a relaxed, confident approach and attitude to life.

This list of essential requirements would also be applicable for other assistance dogs; a sound temperament and willingness to please the handler are the basis of a potentially successful dog.

UNSUITABLE QUALITIES

Dogs with aggressive tendencies in any form (including pure aggression, apprehension or over-protection) are unsuitable as future assistance dogs. Aggression can develop from the threatening, growling stage to actual biting. Possessive behaviour/aggression over food and toys is often seen in young puppies but, if handled carefully, is usually minimal and easily eradicated.

Aggression could be inherited, a breed characteristic, or learned behaviour. In some breeds, it is just part of growing up, a confident young dog challenging his owner's ability to remain in control. A degree of territorial aggression is seen in many dogs – for example, barking at the door when people arrive, and barking when running up and down a boundary. Again, in most dogs, this is easily controlled and it does not develop into anything more serious.

Suspicion is seen as an unacceptable fear reaction to objects, people or situations. It can be the result of insufficient experience, especially if the dog has lacked early socialisation. Suspicion is usually displayed as apprehension – the dog may back away submissively, flatten to the ground, put his ears back, smack his lips, or he may even react in an aggressive way and attack another dog. This behaviour is best described as the apprehensive dog deciding: "I will get you before you get me." With time and further habituation, the problem can often be resolved, otherwise it would be assessed as unacceptable.

Dominant assertive behaviour within the social structure can be shown towards other dogs or people, especially within members of the family. It can also be shown environmentally, as in the case of territorial guarding. This type of dog will display a very confident attitude – on his toes, high tail-carriage, strong eye contact and upright ear-carriage. It is totally unacceptable behaviour in any assistance dog.

CASE HISTORY

ROGER HALL AND ASH

Name: Roger Hall.
Guide Dog: Ash, a Border Collie-Golden Retriever cross, his third Guide Dog.
Family: Married, with two boys.
Occupation/interests: Building and sailing boats.

Roger and Ash – both sea dogs at heart.

" Arriving at Roger's workshop, you are greeted enthusiastically by two dogs. The older dog is Megan, his retired Guide Dog who now lives with Roger's neighbour, who also happens to be his business partner. So Megan still comes to work and is presently teaching Ash a few of her old tricks – stealing the wood, tools and oily rags that Roger keeps close to hand.

Roger and Ash have been working together

for a year now. Roger demonstrates just how settled his partnership has become with Ash through phrases that neither he nor Ash learned at the training centre. The standard phrase to get a Guide Dog to move more quickly is "Hup-up". Roger's more relaxed approach is to say, "Come on, Ash, get a wriggle on", to which Ash immediately responds. To jump a rail, Roger says "Ally up", and Ash clears it like a fence at the Grand National! This rapport, where dog and owner communicate in their own private language, is one of the factors that makes Guide Dog ownership so rewarding.

"My first two dogs were both pure-bred Border Collies. You would be excused for thinking that I have a soft spot for this breed – which I do – but, more importantly, the breed matches my requirements.

"I need a dog that is fairly light in weight and that walks at a brisk pace, as I need to keep up with my children. Not only do I need a dog that is quick to learn new routes but, most importantly, one that can come sailing with me!

"I trained with my first Guide Dog, Andy, in 1981. He was a handsome tri-colour dog, who worked very hard. My original workshop was half-an-hour's walk from home and, thinking

back to those days, we must have done that route more than 5,000 times. Andy loved going sailing and would enthusiastically jump into my arms to be lifted on to the boat. He was very relaxed and content on the boat and enjoyed many sailing trips. He was happy to go on board, sitting up front very much the figurehead. After his death, I decided to scatter his ashes at sea where he had felt so at home.

"Megan, my second dog, was an excellent worker but, sadly, she wasn't so keen on sailing. So I'm delighted that my new dog has got a full set of sea legs!

"My parents were keen sailors, so I've been sailing since I was in a carry-cot. I owned my first boat by the age of 12 and, as with any passion, I learnt all there was to know about boats.

"Registered blind at 17, I was encouraged by teachers and parents to work in a factory as a machine operator. Many blind people were pressured into doing this type of work, but I hated it; so I decided to make a career out of my hobby.

"I now build new boats to order, do a lot of restoration work at the maritime museums in Cardiff and Swansea, and also do repair work on request. For many years, I spent a week each summer, teaching sailing for the Royal Yacht Association Seamanship Foundation.

"I spend most of my day going between the workshop and the marina. I need a dog that can go up and down ladders and on and off boats; one that can quickly learn the different routes around the many marinas I visit in the course of my work. My Guide Dog needs to be quick-witted to suit my personality and temperament, so a Border Collie is ideal.

"When I started training with my new dog, my first impression of Ash was that he was such a big dog, so much taller than Megan, who is very feminine, smaller and lighter-framed.

"When Ash and I went for our first walk together, I also realised just how much Megan had slowed with age, and I found myself back in top gear again.

"Adjusting to a new dog takes time and Ash is very different in temperament to Megan. Before, if Ash made a mistake and I had to correct him, he was more inclined to worry about it, slow up and lose willingness. Megan would just shrug it off and carry on. I had to learn to soften my voice and apply a moderate physical correction for mistakes and quickly praise him as soon as he got it right. This approach quickly restored any lost confidence in Ash and helped me get the best from him.

"My idea of getting away from it all is to take a busman's holiday and go sailing with my wife, children and the dog on Neptune, a traditionally built timber boat. Neptune is moored at the local marina, a 40-minute walk from the workshop, a route that Ash now knows extremely well.

"Apart from coping with the usual hazards of people, traffic, road crossing and loose dogs while working the route to the boat, Ash and I have a variety of obstacles to negotiate once through the security gates at the entrance to the marina. The floating pontoons that divide the mooring areas for boats are open to the water on both left and right, so a central position is essential, for both of us to avoid contact with the sea!

"Having a Guide Dog gives you the freedom to do what you want, when you want. If I have forgotten to measure something that I am repairing on a boat, I can just grab the harness, call my dog, clip the harness on and go. If I didn't have a dog, I would either have to get someone to take me there, or get someone else to do the running around for me. It is this aspect of having a Guide Dog that gives me total independence, which I love and need to keep me sane.

"My family and friends all say I would be like a bear with a sore head if I didn't have a dog. I am a bit hyperactive, always on the go – a little bit like a Border Collie. I reckon that's why we get on so well. '

TRAINING A GUIDE DOG PUPPY

PUPPY-WALKERS
The object of the puppy-walking scheme is to ensure a regular supply of suitable dogs for training as Guide Dogs. This formative year is of vital importance in a puppy's development.

Puppy-walking prospective Guide Dogs has proved to be a major factor in the organisation's success rate, and is widely recognised as fundamental to ensuring the development of acceptable temperamental characteristics.

Puppies are placed in volunteer homes from the age of six weeks. The aim is to rear a puppy in a family environment and for him to be socialised in a variety of situations. The puppy has to be conditioned to all the sights and sounds of a busy town life. Local walks down the road and around the block will gradually be extended to include busy shopping areas and main roads. On these walks, the puppy will encounter adults, children, traffic, shops, and other dogs, together with the sounds and smells that are experienced in these situations.

As the puppy gains experience and confidence, the walker will start to take him into new, busier situations – crowds, large department stores with lifts, steps and slippery floors, etc. Initial over-enthusiasm or caution through lack of experience will be displayed but, with practice and time, the puppy will learn to go up and down stairs steadily, to walk in and out of lifts calmly, and to walk confidently on slippery floors.

The puppy has to be encouraged to ignore the admiring looks and comments they get from passers-by. Many members of the public want to speak to the puppy, especially when they realise it is a Guide Dog puppy. Initially, this is a good opportunity to socialise the pup but, eventually, the puppy starts to look for attention. In extreme cases, he may sit as people approach and demand to be spoken to. This behaviour has to be discouraged before it becomes a habit that stays with them for life.

The puppy has to resist the temptation of scavenging food or rubbish lying on the ground. Often ruled by their stomachs, Labradors can find this very difficult! If allowed to scavenge on a regular basis, they will always be looking for the next opportunity, rather than concentrating on the job in hand.

The puppy also has to be taught to walk at a steady, even pace, just head and shoulders in front of the handler. Going out for a walk is exciting and the pup's pace is initially erratic. Achieving a steady speed, with moderate tension on the lead, takes time. Ignoring any dogs that they may encounter on their leash walks may take even longer.

There are many different situations within the environment that the puppy has to learn to cope with. Regular visits to the railway station or underground train, with the occasional ride, will habituate the puppy to noisy, busy places. These environments also provide access to different types of steps, lifts, footbridges and subways. For example, getting on and off a bus (such a huge step for a young puppy) can be a frightening experience. With the right approach and attitude from the puppy-walker, they soon learn to hop on and off, and to find an empty seat like the rest of us.

The puppy has to learn to walk slightly ahead of the handler and ignore distractions. Voice response, short periods of concentration and control of unacceptable behaviour has to be developed. The natural erratic behaviour patterns of a growing puppy present peaks and troughs in the standard and level of response to the handler, and at certain times more control will be required.

GROWING PAINS

At 16 weeks, the puppy has usually started to produce his adult teeth. This is also a period of development when signs of apprehension may start to show. Regular habituation in varied environments is crucial at this stage, as well as a confident, encouraging attitude from the handler. A sympathetic approach at this stage can convince a puppy who lacks confidence that he is right to be so. A balanced approach of firm voice control but a fair attitude (not expecting too much too

Once the pup is confident in quiet public areas, he is gradually introduced to busier ones.

As part of his socialisation, the puppy is taken to a variety of public places.

soon) will give the puppy the direction he requires to cope with the ongoing habituation and training process.

Puppies between five and seven months of age are likely to test the patience of the most experienced puppy-walkers. The pup's head is growing and changing shape, the adult teeth are now through, but not fully erupted. This can result in bouts of chewing, or more serious destructive behaviour. Increased hormone levels will be reflected in a greater interest shown towards other dogs. Handling this distraction can be difficult in some cases. If the dog is reprimanded by the handler, this negative response can make the dog wary of the handler as well as worried in the presence of other dogs. An overly sympathetic approach, however, can increase the level of dog distraction. The right way of handling this situation is to have an upbeat, positive, firm but fair approach. Also common at this age is a poor response to the "Come" command, especially when enjoying free-exercise.

The third period of change will be seen towards the end of the dog's time with a puppy-walker. A good standard of behaviour and response is often achieved, but the puppy-walker will then often report that the dog's good behaviour seems to be slipping. What the dog now requires is further mental stimulation. This is provided by the dog being returned to the training centre for formal Guide Dog training.

Basic dog handling skills are taught to puppy-walkers. They need to understand:

• Pack hierarchy.
• How to use their voice effectively.
• Timing and use of commands.
• The correct use of equipment provided and of incentives.
• How to develop the dog's willingness and confidence.
• Good lead behaviour.

The puppy-walker needs to house-train the pup and teach him good social behaviour and basic obedience responses. Jumping up at people, getting on furniture, stealing food and barking excessively are all undesirable traits. This period of early training lasts about one year, after which, a gradual improvement in responses, attitude and confidence is looked for. When with a puppy-walker, the puppies are visited and assessed, with help and advice given on a monthly basis by a member of Guide Dogs staff.

For the puppy-walker, it is often a year full of laughter and a few tears, but overall it is a very rewarding experience. Many puppy-walkers go on to face the challenge many more times. This usually improves their ability and skills, producing a better-quality dog each time. Experienced puppy-walkers would be encouraged to take on the more complex breeds, such as the German Shepherd, the Curly Coated Retriever or the Border Collie.

BACK TO THE CENTRE

Once the puppy has returned to the training centre, the puppy-walker receives a written progress report every three months. When the puppy, now an adult, qualifies as a Guide Dog, the puppy-walker is informed and the Association presents them with a colour photograph of the dog in harness with his new owner. The new Guide Dog owner is encouraged to write to the puppy-walker, and many friendships develop from this. If the dog is rejected in training and is not suitable for any other type of work, the puppy-walker is given the opportunity to have the dog back as a pet under the Association's rehoming scheme.

FORMAL GUIDE DOG TRAINING COMMENCES

Guide Dogs for the Blind Association has several training centres throughout the UK. They are all situated near large, urban areas to ensure they are within easy reach of the people that they serve. This is important as it is essential to continue contact with the Guide Dog owner once training is completed.

In the past, most blind people would train with their dog during a residential course. This entailed the Guide Dog owner being away from family and friends for up to four weeks. Unsurprisingly, there is now a move towards home-based or 'domiciliary' training.

It takes just nine months to train a Guide Dog to cope with a variety of situations.

In the future, it is likely that the training the individual receives will be agreed between the instructor and the client. Some people, for instance, prefer to be away from their daily domestic commitments, so they can concentrate on training with their dog. Others enjoy the companionship and mutual support of other people undergoing the same training. Those with young children or elderly dependent parents, generally prefer to be trained at home, with their training fitting in around their other domestic responsibilities.

The average working life of a Guide Dog is seven years and, at present, there are around 4,800 working Guide Dogs in the UK. Once someone has owned a Guide Dog, the organisation has an ongoing commitment to provide replacement dogs for them for as long as they are fit and able to work and care for a dog.

It takes an average of nine months to train a

The 'guiding position' ensures the handler has sufficient time to react to the dog's movements.

The dog is taught to sit at the kerb before being given further instructions.

Guide Dog. Training is based on the willingness of the dog to please his handler. The dog and owner communicate through the harness when working as a team. A comfortable degree of tension through the handle should be sufficient for the handler to feel and interpret the dog's movements. Strong tension can be difficult to follow as the subtleties of movement are lost. Too light a tension means signals received are weak.

The handler should adopt a suitable position alongside the dog in line with his hindquarters. The dog is on the left of the person, with a gap between them of about a hand's width. The dog should have two-thirds of his body length ahead of the handler. This leading or 'guiding position', allows enough time for the handler to react effectively to the dog's movements.

It is essential for the Guide Dog owner to have local knowledge or some idea of the geography of the area in which they are working. It is sufficient for them to know that they have to cross, say,

three roads before making a turn; it is essential that they know whether to make the turn on the up-kerb (the step up from the road on to the kerb) or the down-kerb (the step down from the kerb on to the road) and the approximate distance to their destination. If this is somewhere they have been before, once they think they are within a few yards of their target, they can ask the dog to 'find the door'. Many Guide Dog owners will comment on how impressive their dog's memory can be for places they visited only once many months previously.

Guide Dog owners do not expect their dogs to complete routes unaided. For instance, they would not leave their house saying to the dog: "I want to go to the post office, then the bank and then the chemist." They may, of course, visit these places on a regular basis in the same order, and once the sequence commences, the dog will indicate these places with little input from the owner. It is the ability of the dog to acquire such skills and knowledge that makes Guide Dog mobility so easy and useful for a blind person.

Directional commands (forward, straight on, back, left and right, coupled with following the principle of a straight line from A to B) is the basis of all orientation. Kerbs or the pavement edge are normally the point at which a change of direction would be made, as Guide Dog owners navigate by the numbers of roads crossed. A positive stop, as close as possible to the kerb edge, is essential for accurate safe navigation.

It is the handler at this point who decides the direction of travel. Some blind people find steep up-kerbs hazardous; in this case the dog would stop with its front feet on the up-kerb. The upward movement of the dog's body would give a positive indication to the owner of the presence of the obstacle ahead. Steps up or downwards are indicated and negotiated in the same way.

Developing the guiding position in the young dog takes time. Training the dog to travel at an acceptable speed and to give consistent lead tension is initially encouraged by walking the dog on a long lead. "Hup-up" is the command used to encourage the dog on, and "Steady" is used to slow the dog or maintain a steady pace. Choosing long, straight routes in quiet suburban areas will really encourage the dog to step out. Throughout this stage of training the dog is taught to respond to basic obedience, directional and control commands.

Once the dog is confidently working ahead on the lead, kerb stops, kerb take-offs and turns are gradually introduced. The procedure for turns would be done on the move at a steady pace. Timing the Sit command as the dog is almost in position at the kerb-edge helps to develop an understanding. The whole process can take some time; the dog stopping short or over-shooting the kerb are two of the most common problems at this stage. Handler ability and approach will affect the dog's learning process and attitude to this important aspect of Guide Dog mobility.

The basis of all Guide Dog work is the need to develop the dog's response to control and directional commands in a variety of situations and environments. The Guide Dog owner's ability to control the dog at all times is paramount to the success of the working unit.

BASIC COMMANDS

Sit or Stand
Used to bring the dog to a standstill, to control excessive speed, for the kerb stop, and to control the dog anticipating on a known route.

Down
Used in a social or working situation, e.g. on a bus, train or while queueing in a shop.

Stay
Used in conjunction with the Sit, Stand and Down to maintain a position in either a working or social situation.

Wait
A momentary halt, this command is used to make the dog stand or sit still briefly, e.g. at doors, car obedience, and teaching right shoulder work (see below page 28) in crowds.

Leave/no
Used to control any type of distraction in any situation, e.g. dog, cat, birds, food or people.

Hup-up
Used to encourage forward movement from the dog if speed has slowed or the dog is hesitating to proceed.

Steady
Used to slow the dog's rate of forward progress or maintain a steady speed, e.g. in busy crowded areas, shops, markets and high streets.

DIRECTIONAL COMMANDS

All directional commands are used in conjunction with hand signals and correct body and foot positions.

Forward
Used to initiate the dog's forward movement from a stationary position.

Straight on
Used in many situations, to encourage the dog to stay on or return to a central pavement position and to resume a straight line, e.g. when crossing

'Steady' is the command for the dog to walk at a constant speed, such as when in a busy high street.

Directional commands are given at kerbs to encourage the dog to a specific location.

the road, or, after carrying out a change in direction, to encourage the dog back on to the straight line.

Over/In
'Over' is taught to encourage the dog to move to the left and 'In' is used to encourage the dog to come right. These commands are used to influence the dog's pavement position when teaching or reinforcing obstacle avoidance, otherwise known as 'right shoulder work'.

Right/Left/Back
Directional commands given when the dog is stationary. These commands would be given at the down-kerb or up-kerb and would also be used when directing the dog towards a specific location, such as doors, steps or road crossings.

Any change in direction requires a joint procedure from dog and handler. The handler needs to prepare themselves by distributing their weight and using the correct body and foot positions and hand signals to execute a change in direction or a positive take-off from the down-kerb (forward movement).

OBSTACLE WORK

The dog is taught to maintain a central position on the pavement, moving at a steady speed, in a straight line until commanded to do otherwise. He should only deviate from the straight line if forced to do so. One of the most frequently met hazards for the working Guide Dog and his owner are obstacles. Negotiating these hazards requires a lot of skill on the part of the dog and the handler. This is the unique aspect of Guide Dog mobility which gives blind people that work a Guide Dog greater safety and independence.

Obstacles met can be classified into three kinds:

An obstacle course is set up and the trainee dog is encouraged to find a route through.

- **Solid obstacles** – street signs, lamp-posts, shop displays, letter boxes, scaffolding, cars parked on pavements.
- **Moving obstacles** – pedestrians, pushchairs, bicycles.
- **Off-kerb obstacles** – where the pavement is totally blocked and the dog and handler have to leave the safety of the pavement, step into the road and return to the pavement as soon as it is clear to do so. Examples include road works, over-hanging branches, scaffolding or parked cars. Stepping off the pavement in this way can lead to the blind person becoming disorientated. If the blind person misinterprets the situation, the dog may receive the wrong command and could cross the road instead of negotiating the obstacle.

Obstacle work is taught in two ways, artificially and using the natural hazards met in the environment. When the dog encounters a natural obstacle during training, he will be encouraged to move either "Over" to the left or "In" to the right, giving a wide enough clearance for both dog and handler. It may be necessary for the dog to come to a standstill if the pavement is completely blocked. The trainer will use known areas in the locality to provide this type of training opportunity.

Artificial obstacles are initially taught in the grounds of the training centre. Obstacles are placed in a short row, alternating left and right, and the dog is encouraged to find the route through. There must be sufficient clearance for both dog and handler to get through without either of them touching an obstacle. If the dog fails to give sufficient clearance, the handler must take appropriate action. This could be in the form of a verbal command or hand signal, or by using the lead to encourage the dog to take the most appropriate line. In most cases, a dog is worked on the left-hand side, so the handler's right shoulder is most likely to touch any obstruction when the dog fails to give sufficient clearance. Obstacle avoidance is therefore known as 'right shoulder work'.

The handler's position beside the dog influences him to turn to the left or right or stop for a height obstacle. In the early days, the correct body position of the handler in relation to the dog helps the dog to make the right decision. As the dog shows greater understanding of the task, the handler will reduce the amount of support provided until the dog eventually does it naturally.

The artificial obstacle course provides an intensive repetition of a desired response in a controlled, safe environment, enabling the dog to learn the task efficiently without the usual distractions found in an urban environment. Once the dog has learned the aspects of right shoulder work in the artificial environment, further practice in busier, crowded situations will provide the opportunity for the dog to avoid people, which is the hardest obstacle of them all. Trainers laughingly comment "that some people walk backwards out of shops – sometimes the dog just doesn't have a chance to get it right!"

To reinforce obstacle work they will also train the dogs in quiet areas. Here they will place artificial obstacles. The streets must be chosen carefully, and full co-operation from the local residents is important. Trainers also put up a sign to warn pedestrians what is going on.

TRAFFIC WORK

Traffic work involves teaching a dog to recognise that a moving vehicle within a certain area is a signal to stop. It is very difficult to teach properly and for the Guide Dog owner to maintain the desired response without putting themselves at risk.

It is the responsibility of the Guide Dog to decide when it is safe to cross the road; if they are not able to make this decision, they should gain assistance. The public perception that the dog can cope with any traffic conditions and that the dog makes the decision to cross the road is mistaken.

A sensitive dog will probably show more natural awareness of traffic, which can, with care, be usefully channelled during traffic training. The more confident, resilient type of dog may need the car horn to be sounded during traffic training to make him more aware of the oncoming vehicle.

The dog is taught either to remain at the kerb edge or to stop in the road if a vehicle comes within a critical distance of the dog and handler. This procedure is taught both naturally and artificially. Using natural traffic opportunities that occur during a training walk will give the trainer a chance to teach the dog to be disobedient under certain circumstances. The dog is expected to ignore the "Forward" command at the kerb edge when a car is approaching. If the dog is already in the road and a vehicle approaches, the dog is also taught to stop and subsequently ignore any

Traffic work can be practised on an ordinary training walk.

If a vehicle approaches while they cross the road, the dog is taught to stop.

After being taught to sit at the kerb, the 'forward' instruction is given.

attempts by the handler to encourage the dog to move forward.

Artificial traffic training is undertaken in a quiet area. Another experienced trainer will drive a vehicle on a set route, giving the dog and handler repeated opportunity to practise the procedures for traffic coming from the left or right.

Guide Dogs for the Blind still emphasises to all Guide Dog owners that the advice they have been given during training about traffic is that they, not the dog, are the decision-makers, when it comes to crossing the road. A dog has very limited understanding of the dangers of traffic and to expect a dog to shoulder this responsibility is unrealistic. You may have observed street dogs avoiding oncoming vehicles. This is probably because they have been struck once or more, and an association with a vehicle causing pain has produced a conditioned response.

TRAINING THE TRAINERS

All Guide Dog organisations around the world have difficulty in recruiting and keeping good training staff. The variable qualities that are required to be successful in this job are often hard to find in one person. They need strength to cope with the physical demands of the job and yet be sufficiently mentally sensitive to empathise when training the blind person with the dog. Training a Guide Dog is not comparable with taking a dog for a walk in the woods. The daily demands of working different dogs in an urban environment, with all the related urban aggravations, is exhausting and requires stamina.

It is easy to glamorise the job. People who dream of an outdoor job working with animals often apply to become Guide Dog trainers and instructors believing they will simply be walking dogs all day! Guide Dog trainers/instructors do not *walk* dogs, they *work* them, and this is not a job for those who cannot stand the rain. Training goes on whatever the weather because Guide Dog owners who go to work or have children to take to school have to go whatever the weather!

Patience is another quality. Training dogs and people is repetitive work that can be boring or frustrating. There will often be dips in the dog's performance. The new owner will be less aware of

Being a Guide Dog trainer involves working in all weathers – but the rewards are great.

how the dog is behaving, especially in distracting situations, and the instructor has to be patient and accept the limitations imposed by visual impairment.

However well-trained, the dog will only achieve the standard set by the new owner. Guide Dog owners have Guide Dogs not because they are dog trainers or have a particular interest in dog training, but because they have a need for mobility. There will, therefore, be a huge range of abilities among the people that an instructor has to train.

GUIDE DOG TRAINERS

When the puppy has completed his puppy-walking phase, he is returned to the regional training centre for assessment and further training.

The trainer will assess the dog's temperament and progress achieved on the puppy-walking scheme, with habituation to the environment and various situations. He will also assess the dog's response to the basic obedience and control commands, progress on straight-line training, and capacity to concentrate.

In the initial weeks of training, the trainer will concentrate on developing greater understanding of the straight line procedure, pavement position, introduction to kerb stops, directional turns, and control for distractions, and will develop longer periods of concentration. The dogs will be encouraged to walk ahead on a long lead. The handler only moves up to the dog's shoulder when approaching hazards such as kerbs, steps or obstacles.

This is the first difficult period of transition the young dog will experience. Moving from the comfort of a home environment and the individual attention provided by the puppy-walker into a kennel environment can have a dramatic effect on the dog's behaviour and temperament.

Like children exposed to university life for the first time, without the influence of their family, it can cause two reactions. They will either become quiet and withdrawn or adopt a wild and extrovert approach. During this period of adjustment young dogs in kennels for the first time experience similar reactions.

The majority, of course, fall somewhere between these two extremes, but the influence of this change of environment must be acknowledged and taken into account by the trainer when starting to train the young dog. For example, there may be an increase in the use of nose for sniffing walls and posts, and a consequent loss of concentration, with the additional distraction of wind scenting.

Dog distraction will also probably show an increase, to the extent of becoming a chronic problem in some dogs. These early transitional problems usually disappear after two to six weeks, or at least diminish considerably.

Also at the back of the Guide Dog trainer's and instructor's mind is the knowledge that he or she has a set number of weeks allowed in which to train the dog. This places enormous pressure on them – mistakes can be made, taking valuable time to put right.

During the first few weeks of training, the dog will be fitted with the body-piece section of the harness. This is made of leather and most dogs adapt quickly to wearing it. At first, it is difficult for a puppy to accept wearing a collar. In the same way, an adult dog may find it difficult to accept wearing the harness. Accepting the harness is made easier if the trainer ensures it fits correctly. A common mistake with equipment is to assume that one harness, handle, collar or check chain fits all. This is rather like the military approach to uniform and is just as unsuccessful. It is essential that the correct size of harness and type of collar is chosen for the individual dog. A check chain is not always the best option; a leather collar or half-check may be more suitable.

Training sessions usually last around half an hour twice daily and all training exercises need to be repeated. As the dog's understanding and confidence develop, the trainer will repeat the exercises in busier areas. Such areas might include railway stations and bus stations at busy times of travel and street markets on popular days. These situations provide more noise and distractions – all aspects of urban life that the dog must learn to ignore. Once the dog responds correctly with minimal prompting from the trainer to situations in any environment, a more advanced approach can be adopted.

The handle will now be attached to the harness.

It takes years of specialist training to become a Guide Dog mobility instructor.

This represents a significant change for the dog and its relationship with the trainer. Care should be taken not to put on the harness in such a way as to cause a negative response. The dog must enjoy wearing the harness, and clumsy dropping of the handle at this stage could cause the dog some concern. The trainer/instructor needs to be aware of the possible effects and make allowances for the dog and its behavioural reactions until accustomed to working in full harness.

GUIDE DOG MOBILITY INSTRUCTORS

There are as many methods of training a Guide Dog as there are Guide Dog trainers. Even within the large schools, with established methods and procedures, there is inevitably scope for individuals to adopt methods and techniques which suit their own personal approach to training both dogs and people.

It takes three years to qualify as a Guide Dog mobility instructor in the UK. It takes this long because the instructor not only has to train dogs

in specialist tasks, but also teach visually impaired people how to handle and work with their dogs. This requires knowledge of human psychology and how people learn. Teaching Guide Dog skills to individuals whose age can range from 18 to 80 requires a particular blend of empathy, enthusiasm and energy.

Instructors must also be able to impart advanced standards of instruction to Guide Dogs in training, so a comprehensive knowledge and understanding of canine psychology is essential. In the same way that Guide Dog owners vary enormously in age and ability, so dogs available for training range in type. Because instructors have to achieve the desired result in the allocated time, they must have a number of methods at their disposal. What is suitable with one dog may not achieve the same results with another.

Trainee instructors must train a number of Guide Dog/owner partnerships and sit tough examinations before qualifying. They are assessed at every stage of their training. This mixture of practical and theoretical testing provides a series of hurdles which every instructor has to clear successfully. The reason for this is that qualified instructors have the safety of the visually impaired people in their hands; the reduction of the possibilities of error is paramount.

As well as training dogs and people, the instructor must assess the suitability of applicants who apply for Guide Dogs and be able to offer support to those owners who are experiencing problems with their Guide Dog work.

The mobility instructor will complete the advanced stage of training with the dog. He will continue with the process of consolidation of skills, assessment of the dog ready for matching with the blind person, and finally the training of the blind person with the dog.

During advanced training, blindfold work will be practised. This is where the trainer or instructor will watch a blindfolded colleague to see if the dog is working adequately. This indicates how the dog behaves without any cues from the handler, as even the most experienced instructor acknowledges that it is difficult to avoid giving subtle signals. For example, a blindfolded person is likely to walk into an obstacle if led there by the dog, but a sighted person – who can see it coming – may hold back a little, walk slower and so on, passing on these signals to the dog.

Blindfold work is also an opportunity to check how the dog responds to less accurate following. Tripping and stumbling are common problems for the new Guide Dog owner, who is learning to adjust to this form of mobility. Blindfold walks would be practised with the support of another instructor. Some Guide Dog schools use a local Guide Dog owner to work the dog for the same purpose.

MATCHING THE DOG AND OWNER

In the later stages of training, the dog is matched to a suitable blind person. Each applicant's medical history is different as there are numerous eye conditions that can cause impaired vision. Some occur more frequently, such as cataracts, retinal detachment, macular dystrophy, genetic eye disease and injury. There are, of course, many others too numerous to list. Those applying for a Guide Dog may have health conditions in addition to visual impairment. Epilepsy, hearing loss, diabetes, angina, and old age are some of the common health problems that have to be taken into consideration when assessing the applicant's suitability for training, or when matching the individual with a dog.

It is not just the applicant's physical fitness, health, and level of independent mobility that are assessed for suitability – home and work circumstances are all recorded and a decision is made accordingly. Their motivation and previous dog handling experience also have to be taken into consideration.

It is important to explain the responsibilities of what dog ownership entails, as many people will not have owned a dog before. The dog must make a positive contribution to their life and, for some individuals, the responsibility of dog ownership outweighs the benefits.

Once the matching decision has been made, training requirements specific to the individual's needs can be practised. For example, owners who commute may need a dog which requires additional training on buses, trains or underground railway systems, especially during

The applicant's lifestyle must be assessed in order to find a suitable dog. For example, an owner who regularly uses the bus will need a dog who has had extra training in this area.

busy periods. If the dog is destined to be owned by a teacher, experience of large numbers of children in a school environment is essential. If someone is a music enthusiast, then experience of concert halls and applause, to which some dogs can react badly, has to be taught.

It is important to match the capabilities of the client with the ability of the dog. In the UK, a lot of Guide Dog owners will have met their dog before arriving at the training centre. Matching visits are now carried out, where the dog is taken to the new owner's home to check that the dog is suitable for the individual concerned. Some Guide Dog owners will meet their dog only after they have been at the centre for a few days.

This first encounter can be very emotional. After formal introductions and a reminder of a few do's and don'ts, the dog and owner are left alone to get to know each other.

TRAINING THE NEW PARTNERSHIP

For someone who has never owned a dog before, getting to know the Guide Dog can be stressful. Meeting the new dog can be a time of mixed emotions also for owners given replacement

Guide Dogs after their old dog retired or was lost through ill-health.

It is important that the dog settles and forms an attachment with his new owner as quickly as possible. The dog will now be the new owner's constant companion. The more time spent with the dog on a one-to-one basis in their bedroom, going for free exercise in the grass runs at the centre, grooming, feeding, and generally being in contact with the dog, will speed up the process of the dog transferring his affections from the instructor to the new owner.

Training the dog with the client can take up to four weeks. The flexibility of the residential course allows for the variety of client ability. The rate of progress will depend on the aptitude of the owner and the dog's acceptance of the change of handler and circumstances.

The new Guide Dog owner will be taught how to handle the dog in any situation they are likely to encounter in their future working life together. The blind person also has to learn how to handle the dog, on and off the lead and while in harness. For a blind person, especially those who have been blind since birth, walking unassisted in a straight line can be very difficult. Understanding the spatial concept of turning left and right from this straight direction can also cause confusion. It is therefore essential that the dog is taught to carry out these turns in an accurate fashion to give a positive indication of direction.

To avoid the relationship being damaged through mishandling, the new owner and trainer will go through the procedures of alignment to the dog, harness commands, handler's position and use of voice, artificially. This procedure is called 'handle walks'. The trainer takes the role of the dog, and the blind person has the opportunity to practise all procedures and handling techniques without causing any stress to the dog. Even experienced Guide Dog owners will practise handle walks to correct any lapses in technique they might have acquired over the years with their previous dog.

While it is a difficult time for the new owner, it is also a testing time for the dog. Transferring his affections from the trainer to his new owner can be very stressful. The instructor has the difficult task of ignoring the dog's attempts to make

New owners soon learn to trust their dog's judgements and to walk confidently with their new companions.

contact, avoiding eye contact and ensuring that it is the new owner that praises the dog's good behaviour, not the trainer.

As with any new relationship, the dog goes through a period, during the training time, of testing the owner. This could be in the form of poor social behaviour, getting on the furniture, jumping up, poor response to recall, or bumping the Guide Dog owner into obstacles. Repeating exercises and obedience sessions usually help to resolve these problems.

The Guide Dog owner is taught basic dog psychology, as it is important that they understand how the dog thinks and why he reacts in the way he does. They are also taught feeding, grooming and general care procedures. Every aspect of dog ownership is covered so that the Guide Dog owner is as confident as possible about the new partnership.

When the Guide Dog owner returns home with their new dog, their instructor will visit them to practise the routes they do regularly, e.g. to work, to school, to the shops, use of transport and road crossings within their local area, as well as finding new routes that are more suitable for the working unit to make use of.

It is important to ensure the safety and confidence of the dog and the owner in their new role together. All owners are visited on an annual basis, throughout the dog's working life. More frequent visits will be made if required and towards the end of the dog's working life.

CASE HISTORY

DAVID BLUNKETT AND LUCY

Name: Rt Hon. David Blunkett.
Guide Dog: Lucy, a Curly Coated Retriever-Labrador cross.
Family: Three children.
Occupation/interests: Secretary of State for Education and Employment and MP for Sheffield Brightside.

' Born with very limited sight, which gradually deteriorated, David can now only discern strongly contrasted light and dark. His visual impairment has not stopped him reaching great political heights, however. An increasing involvement in local politics led to him eventually becoming a Member of Parliament, then Shadow Health Secretary, and finally a Cabinet Minister when Labour was elected into power in 1997.

David has a hectic work schedule, with consecutive meetings held in opposite ends of the Palace of Westminster, or, indeed at

Having a Guide Dog has helped David to overcome many of the obstacles caused by his blindness.
Photo: Mirror Group.

opposite ends of the country. With the help of a Guide Dog, David is able to overcome many obstacles to ensure his blindness does not hinder his demanding work.

Bonding with a Guide Dog can also be time-consuming and involve considerable hard work. And, since a Guide Dog's working life is not as long as that of its owner, relationships need to be built each time a new dog is taken on.

David has worked with four Guide Dogs: Ruby, Teddy, Offa, and now Lucy (who are all remembered in his autobiography *On a Clear Day*). Each one has made the headlines in their own right. Ruby, a Labrador, hit the news after she was barred access to the Palace of Westminster while accompanying David on a visit as part of his university politics course. The uproar resulted in the authorities relenting and so, in due course, Ruby made history by becoming the first dog to set paw in the Palace of Westminster.

Teddy, a Curly Coated Retriever-Labrador cross, was the first dog to be allowed on the floor of the Commons Chamber when David was first elected a Member of Parliament in 1987, and Offa, a German Shepherd-Golden Retriever cross, was the first dog to be televised in the House of Commons. Lucy, a Curly Coated Retriever-Labrador cross, is the first Guide Dog to sit by the government benches.

Ruby
"a lively, mischievous and outrageous blonde"

'It had never been my intention to acquire a guide dog. Throughout my teens, I had come across guide dogs or heard people speaking about them, usually, but not exclusively, in highly sentimental terms. I felt this presented the wrong image, and that a guide dog's work as an aid to independence, dignity and mobility should be of more crucial importance.

"Finally I decided that, if I were to accept the challenge of a place at Sheffield University and a growing involvement in politics, it would be helpful to be able to move around

freely without having to rely on other people or on my own nervous energy and mobility skills.

"In September 1969, I was introduced to Ruby, a Labrador, who was to be my companion for the best part of nine years. Deftly our instructor encouraged Ruby to transfer her affection and loyalty from him to me, and calmed my anxiety when inexperience led to incorrect handling. Day by day, my sense of freedom grew as I learned to be guided by Ruby. It was a tremendously exhilarating experience – I had never before felt so liberated.

"Ruby's ability to steal food while on the harness was legendary. All too frequently, as I later found out, people were too polite to let me know what she was doing. During a camping holiday, friends informed me she had eaten their bacon and eggs straight out of the frying pan. As for the tea trolleys which constantly circulated the council offices, the trays of cakes and iced buns on their lower shelves were seldom safe from Ruby's depredations. Nothing was. If she were off the lead anywhere in the vicinity of the dustbin, she would be in there like a shot, head down inside, rooting in the depths for scraps, while her bottom and tail waggled obscenely in the air.

"No dog of mine was ever again allowed to behave in like manner, though I had to ask myself how much of the blame was mine for allowing misbehaviour during Ruby's crucial first months with me at home.

"By the time she reached the ripe old age of ten, Ruby had developed a limp – arthritis. It was time for her to retire as soon as a suitable replacement could be found. Fortunately, Ruth [David's then wife] was at home much of the time with Alistair [David's son], and we were able to keep Ruby with us. Once she realised she no longer had to work, the arthritis was much improved. She resumed all her old habits of escaping over the garden wall and burrowing in dustbins, scavenging scraps until she blew up into a barrel shape.

"When my new guide dog, Teddy, arrived home with me, Ruby behaved like a grumpy old lady. She was thoroughly tetchy towards him, until she found that he was out with me most of the time, and then she relented somewhat.

"When she finally succumbed at the age of 16, I was deeply saddened by her death. Although she may not have been loyal and reliable, and would certainly have won no medals as Guide Dog of the year, she had affectionately given me considerable service. We had been through some difficult and testing times together – not all of them Ruby's fault! **,**

' Meeting Teddy was an amazing experience. Here was a dog who did not shed golden hairs all over the carpet, furniture or my trousers. Here was a dog who took a genuine interest in where I wanted to go. My sort of dog.

Offa was a dog who lived life in the fast lane, so adapted well to David's hectic lifestyle. Photo: Mirror Group.

"I had learned the lessons of the previous ten years and was careful to ensure that I followed the rules imposing maximum discipline tempered by affection and praise.

"In May 1980, I was elected Leader of Sheffield City Council. One of my duties as Leader of Sheffield City Council was to meet visiting dignitaries. Among our most memorable guests at the Town Hall were the Queen and Prince Philip, who were to mingle fairly informally with local figures over a cup of tea.

"As the Queen moved round the room, I waited pensively. Teddy, with his long legs and magisterial bearing, had no such polite inhibitions. As the Queen approached, in the belief that the cup in the Queen's hand was being offered to him, Teddy thrust his head forward to take a look. There followed a momentary flurry of activity. The Queen hastily withdrew her cup and calamity was avoided by a whisker. The Queen, being an experienced dog owner, was perfectly equal to the situation.

"Teddy's behaviour at the royal tea party was a forgivable lapse in his otherwise exemplary behaviour. Unlike Ruby, he caused me remarkably few moments of anxiety in the course of what was, for a Guide Dog, an exceptionally long and demanding existence.

"With my election as an MP, Teddy was set to become the first dog allowed on the floor of the Commons' Chamber proper. There was, however, a dark cloud hanging over us: Teddy's declining health due to old age. Could he withstand the long hours and pressure of my first year in Parliament? Even at the age of 11, his commitment and loyalty made him as eager as ever for work. It was deeply touching.

"Then one hot humid day in May, I noticed that Teddy was panting, not abnormally at first, but as the day faded and the air temperature dropped, he seemed to grow much worse.

"Teddy's heart and liver were failing – he had only a few weeks to live. I dropped everything and took Teddy by train back to Sheffield. There I left him with friends, who I knew would love and care for him. I reluctantly returned to London, where I tried my best to concentrate on the tasks in hand. It was not easy.

"On July 5, as the House of Commons was debating a motion, I was given the message that Teddy had been rushed to the vet after collapsing and losing the use of his legs. The vet felt that he had come to the end of the road and that it would be kinder to put him to sleep. I had to return home at once. Without waiting for permission to be absent from the vote, I caught the next train.

"I have to admit that on that evening, with all the memories of Teddy flooding back, I became the sentimentalist I had so scorned in others 20 years earlier, before I had a dog.

"In the days following Teddy's death, many kind friends and colleagues expressed their condolences, but none was more unexpected than a handwritten message from Margaret Thatcher saying how sorry she was that Teddy had died and that she understood what a great loss it would be for me, not only for practical reasons, but also for the loss of the enormous affection Guide Dogs have for their owners. I never had the opportunity to debate politics with Margaret Thatcher, but she did have a passing acquaintance with Teddy and would always pat him on the head when she passed, so perhaps her letter should not have come as a surprise. Iron Lady she might have been, but she did have a soft spot for Teddy.

"Teddy had become equally widely known outside Parliament and so many sacks of letters arrived from sympathetic members of the public that a fund was set up in his memory. This raised over £7,600 for the Guide Dogs for the Blind Association and helped provide training for several new Guide Dogs, one of whom was to be named Teddy. I'm sure 'the gentle giant' would have liked that since he had no sons of his own. **,**

David with Lucy outside the Palace of Westminster.
Photo: Mirror Group.

Offa
"a lively dog, full of bounce"

' Taking on a new dog is not as easy as it might appear. Although basically the same, each trainer has different techniques, while, of course, each dog has its own individual temperament. On top of which, I had acquired some bad habits over the years with Ruby and Teddy, and these needed to be eliminated or modified when dealing with a new dog – rather like someone who has been driving for ten years having to retake a driving test.

"So it was that in August 1988 I attended the training centre to meet my new partner, Offa. I could not have wished for a more lively dog, full of bounce. Everyone at the centre thought Offa was wonderful, certainly one of their favourites. Becoming accustomed to him as a Guide Dog was, however, a different matter. Like Teddy in his youth, Offa seemed to have inbuilt booster rockets which meant he would shoot off at a rate of knots with me clinging for dear life to the harness, trying to slow him down. I was out of practice and had to rediscover muscles long out of use.

"While we were training, I discovered Offa's fascination for smaller animals – especially furry ones. Offa's trainer recently reminded me of the day a television crew arrived to interview me about my new dog. In the course of the recording, Offa became transfixed by the fur cover on the large microphone, which, being a novice in such matters, at that time, he evidently mistook for an animal. As soon as the microphone was pushed under my nose, Offa started to creep towards it and then began to bark, to the great consternation of the camera crew and the sound recordist. A brief training session followed to ensure that it did not happen again.

"Offa's most appealing aspects were undoubtedly his willingness to do the job and his keen desire to please, both of which had a tendency to lead to the over-zealous response. For instance, if I said, 'Find the door', he would find it at 50 miles per hour. He was highly possessive and liked to be the centre of attention, a trait typical of the German Shepherd in him. If someone else appeared to be attracting too much notice from me, he would grow jealous and try to impose himself upon me. The interesting thing was that he could obviously distinguish between work and leisure because this behaviour was never apparent in the House.

"I was very fond of Offa, but recognised very early in the partnership that spoiling him or indulging him too much would lead to difficulties; I had to be kind and fair – but firm.

"During the General Election in 1992, Offa suffered a terrible occurrence of stomach torsions – which sometimes kills large dogs. The vet, Paddy March, saved his life by a whisker. Thanks to Paddy March and the enormous genius which he brought to bear, Offa recovered, but due to my heavy responsibilities (including taking on the chairmanship of the Party), we were spending more time than ever travelling the country. Offa was beginning to show that he had had enough and was ready to retire – a reluctance

to enter the House as the week progressed and lack of enthusiasm for the harness.

"Paddy March and his family fostered Offa from 1994 to his death just before his thirteenth birthday on June 27, 1999.

"Guide Dogs for the Blind was finding it harder than expected to find a replacement of the same calibre as Offa. They considered a lovely Golden Retriever-collie cross – a mini version of Offa. I liked him very much when we tried him round the Houses of Parliament and in the surrounding streets, but our partnership was not to be. The very next day he took off after a cat while on harness and had to be taken back to the centre for further training. I will always wonder whether Offa had a quiet word in his ear when they were romping together in St James's Park – 'I should blot your copybook and get out pretty damn quick, if I were you, unless you want to suffer the House of Commons, day in, day out for the next eight years or so.'

> ### Lucy
> "a dog you cannot help but love, and, in practical Guide Dog terms, probably the best of the lot."

'Lucy turned out to be a delightful smaller version of Teddy. As a test run, her informal introduction to the House of Commons could not have been more auspicious. I sneaked her into the Chamber behind the Speaker's Chair, where we settled ourselves in the nearest available space on the front bench rather than in my usual place. I could feel her head turning from side to side as she took in everything around her.

"There was a great deal of noise and commotion in the House that day as it was Prime Minister's Questions, but Lucy eventually settled down contentedly. Scarcely had she done so, however, when furore erupted as a Tory MP called upon John Major to resign over a row concerning voting percentages in the expanded European Union. There was pandemonium throughout the Chamber as MPs of every persuasion shouted, booed, clapped and waved order papers. I kept my hand on Lucy's head to reassure her and check she was not in any distress, but she remained oblivious to the mayhem around us.

"When Lucy arrived at my home in Sheffield, she explored every nook and cranny of her new garden. Within a very short time the lawn was littered with sticks which she had retrieved from the hedge and tossed into the air in her enjoyment.

"Yet the moment the harness was put on, she would become calm and mature, recognising that she had a job to do. Lucy and I took to each other immediately. During our first weekend together, we concentrated on attempting to achieve in four days what would normally require three weeks in a training centre. She appeared relaxed with family and friends, and generally assumed her role with amazing ease.

"Despite the House being in recess, we had a hectic schedule of meetings, speeches and press conferences as well as further campaigning visits around the country. There was no time to break Lucy in gently as the tempo of work increased. In addition to the Local and European Elections, the leadership contest was gathering momentum. Since John Smith's death, all my endeavours as Chairman had been focused on how to draw everyone together within the Party in order to prevent its disintegration.

"Despite having entered the Chamber several times with Lucy to accustom her to the Labour front bench, when the day came for our first formal appearance together, she made her own decision. Labour's recent success in the European elections had led her to believe that we had taken over government and she thought a brisk walk to the Government despatch box was called for.

"Helpful Labour colleagues hastily came to the rescue and at the last minute redirected us to the Labour front bench. Afterwards when people remarked that Lucy had taken me to the wrong side of the Chamber, I replied that she had in fact taken me to the right side, but a couple of years too soon!"

"Meanwhile I wondered what the political future might hold in store for me. If the incident which had occurred on the floor of the House of Commons was anything to go by, then the auguries for the future were favourable. ,

2 HEARING DOGS

Ours is a noisy world, and peace and quiet is valued by many for its rarity. The silence of deafness, however, can lead to a life of loneliness. Deafness can make others think an individual is rude or disinterested as there is no outward sign of hearing loss. Being deaf may mean not responding to a "Good morning" or "Can I help?" if the speaker is stood alongside or behind the deaf person, who is not aware that they are being spoken to. Deafness can therefore lead to a life of loneliness, isolation and solitary existence.

Technology has been used very successfully to improve communication for deaf people. Flashing lights on telephones, vibrotactile devices and modern hearing aids all help. The charity Hearing Dogs for Deaf People offers something more than cutting-edge technology. It provides dogs which offer help and companionship, security and friendship and an aid which is easily understood by the public.

Hearing Dogs for Deaf People owe their success not just to the abilities of their dogs or the skill of their trainers, but to the wonderful warm bond which develops between these dogs and their owners. This bond is so tangible it can almost be touched. It grows so well because of the ancient interdependence between man and dog, and this makes an enormous difference to the lives of so many deaf people.

HISTORY OF THE HEARING DOG

The idea of training dogs to assist deaf people originated in America. In 1976, the parents of a deaf girl requested help. They wanted to give their daughter greater independence while providing the feeling of security and companionship. 'The Hearing Ears' scheme was introduced, supported by the American Humane Association. The process quickly gathered momentum, training dogs to alert their owners to specific sounds within the home or in public buildings.

Lady Wright, Vice President of the Royal

Many different types of dog are used as Hearing Dogs – though most are small to medium-sized.

National Institute for the Deaf and Dr Bruce Fogle, a veterinary surgeon, discussed the possibility of introducing something similar in the UK. It took three years for a small group of enthusiastic people to promote the idea enough to gain sufficient financial support to launch a three-year pilot scheme in 1982.

The first dog to be trained was called Favour, a rescue dog from the National Canine Defence League. Favour was trained as a demonstration dog and travelled the country with his trainer/handler Tony Blunt, now Chief Executive of Hearing Dogs for Deaf People.

The training of the dogs started from the home of Gillian Lacey in Chinnor, Oxfordshire. She was the scheme's first placement counsellor. In April 1983, a dog called Lady became the first Hearing Dog to qualify with Eileen Sullivan from Westcliffe-On-Sea, in Essex. Since then, 460 dogs have been trained and placed with deaf owners in the UK.

Rescue dog Favour, the first to be trained as a Hearing Dog.

CASE HISTORY

JOYCE LEONARD AND CLANCY

Name: Joyce Leonard.
Hearing Dog: Clancy, Jack Russell Terrier.
Occupation/interests: Housewife. Fund-raises for Hearing Dogs.
Family: Married with five children, seven grandchildren and three great-grandchildren.

Joyce and her husband, Gordon, have been married for 55 years. They both coped well with Joyce's loss of hearing.

' I am totally deaf in my left ear and I only have 35 per cent hearing ability in my right ear. The day I realised I needed some sort of help was when Gordon was rushed into hospital for emergency treatment for a heart attack. I was shocked because I hadn't heard him when he was taken ill in the night.

"I found myself alone and feeling very vulnerable. You never think of losing your partner until something like this happens. It made us sit down and talk, which led to us discussing the possibilities of me applying for a Hearing Dog.

"We have always had a pet dog. We enjoy the companionship that a dog can give, and, apart from the support a Hearing Dog would provide me, it would get us both out walking again: regular exercise, doctors orders!

"I was interviewed by a member of the Hearing Dogs staff. They wanted to know all about me and my lifestyle. How often I go shopping? Do I work, and, if so, would I want to take the dog to work with me? Was I a member of any club? Did the grandchildren visit regularly? They also asked me questions about my previous dog experience, and, if my application was successful, did I have a preference for a particular breed?

"I had owned terriers for more than 40

Clancy has a terrific sense of fun, and gives considerable companionship to Joyce.

years, so I was a bit biased towards a terrier. I also had to have a hearing test. Once the formalities were over, I was delighted when they informed me I had been accepted and would be put on the waiting list until a suitable dog was found. The waiting was the worst part. I was lucky they found me a dog quite quickly; some people have to wait up to two years. Seven months was more than long enough for me.

"Gordon also came to the centre when we were invited for the initial week's training. We stayed in one of the training houses. The interior layout had been altered. It was now a simulated floor plan of our own home. In the bedroom, the alarm clock was the same as mine at home and the telephones were the same type and in the same place. We took our own food and linen – it was a bit like packing to go on holiday to a self-catering unit. But instead of being excited, I had a few butterflies in my stomach!

"The whole week was planned out for us. Each day consisted of two sound training sessions, an obedience session, a trip to town and a walk with the dog to practise recall and retrieve. Gordon was with me to concentrate on the cooking and keeping the house tidy. I could then focus completely on my new dog, a Jack Russell called Clancy.

"The person that trains the dog is not the person that trains you how to use him to his full potential. A placement officer completes the week's training at the centre and then visits you regularly at home. The idea of the placement officer being a 'stranger' is to encourage the dog to quickly form a bond and therefore work for the recipient rather than work for the person the dog was trained by.

"Clancy's reaction to three strangers in the house was to ignore us all! She went through the motions of the sound tasks she had been taught, willingly but not enthusiastically. It wasn't until we went for walk on the first evening we saw the real Clancy. The trainer suggested we took Clancy on her favourite route to see if that would perk her up. It certainly did – from then on, we didn't look back! Clancy is now my shadow; wherever I go, she usually comes too.

"We have had lots of fun together. She is a wonderful companion, as well as providing me with such valuable practical help. My husband says I am a lot more confident since I have had Clancy. She has learned the sounds that occur regularly. The difference between the front door bell and the back door knocker. She jumps on to the bed and nibbles my ear when the alarm clock rings in the morning.

"Clancy is very useful at meal-times. When I have cooked the dinner and it is on the table

Having owned terriers for more than 40 years, it came as no surprise that Joyce's Hearing Dog was a Jack Russell Terrier.

waiting, I can send Clancy to fetch my husband. Off she goes to alert Gordon by jumping up at him, and the two of them soon reappear.

"The role was soon to be reversed. Gordon, while outside gardening one day, slipped and fell into our pond. Although not seriously hurt, he was badly bruised and extremely shaken by the experience. But worse still, he couldn't get out of the pond. It was no use shouting for my help – I was indoors, oblivious to Gordon's plight. So he sent Clancy to fetch me, which she did. In fact, she was frantic, scrabbling at my legs to alert me. I asked her 'what is it?' and Clancy rushed off, so I followed her. She led me out into the garden where I found Gordon lying in the pond. If it wasn't for Clancy, he could have been stranded there for a lot longer. Wet, cold and very smelly!

"Clancy has changed my life. I hated being on my own. Now, if Gordon goes out, I feel I can still communicate with the outside world. I no longer miss the telephone ringing or leave visitors standing on the doorstep, their arrival unheard. Gordon has to eat less burnt offerings, thanks to my wonderful little dog. She's a wonderful ambassador for Hearing Dogs, and a reliable friend to me. **,**

SOURCE OF SUPPLY

Three-quarters of Hearing Dogs are from rescue centres. Using dogs from such a source is another aspect of the charity's work that is so inspiring. These otherwise unwanted dogs, usually dumped for no fault of their own, are given a chance to do a worthwhile job.

The organisation will consider almost any type of dog – anything from the largest to the smallest, pedigree or mongrel, as long as they do not exceed three years of age. The dog's most important attribute must be that he has a friendly, responsive disposition. A dog with an independent, aloof character would be avoided.

A lot of time is spent regularly contacting the vast number of rescue centres around the country. Staff constantly remind them that the charity is always on the look-out for suitable dogs. Breed

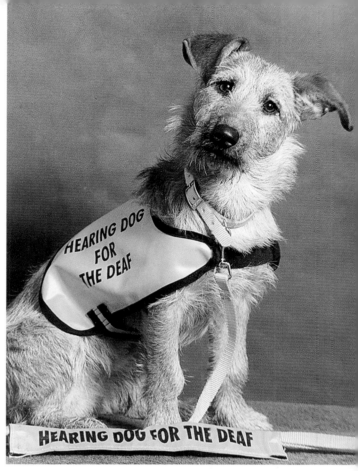

Most dogs are chosen from rescue centres and are often crossbreeds and mongrels.

rescue societies are another source. Re-homing co-ordinators often offer suitable dogs, or suggest to owners that they offer them to the Hearing Dogs' training programme.

Once a puppy or adult dog has been selected for training he is taken directly to a puppy socialiser's home. This avoids bringing the dog into the kennel environment at the training centre. Risk of transferring infections from one kennel environment to another has to be avoided. It is also less stressful for the dog to keep the number of environment and handler changes to a minimum.

PUPPY SOCIALISERS

The puppy socialiser will home the dog for anything from two to nine months, depending on the age and development of the individual. As with Dogs for the Disabled and Guide Dogs, the puppy socialiser of a future Hearing Dog plays a vital role in the development of the dog.

Early socialisation and training is required to develop the potential of the dog. The future owner may need to take the dog into a variety of situations. Habituating the dog to all the sights and sounds of everyday life is essential. Traffic, people, crowds, shops, bus and train travel are all aspects of the socialiser's job to educate the dog. The puppy socialiser will teach the basic obedience responses of sit, down, stay and come, as well as introducing the first sound response reaction. The same will be taught to an adult rescue dog – staff assume the dogs have had no training/socialisation and so start from scratch.

The dog is encouraged to 'come' and make contact with the socialiser when it hears the squeaker. Early introduction to sound response identifies the dog's future potential as a successful Hearing Dog.

The dog is taught to respond to the sound of the whistle. The basics start while the dog is at home with the socialiser. At meal-times, the dog will be taught to sit and wait while the food bowl is placed on the floor. The dog is not allowed to move forward and start to eat until two blasts on the whistle are heard. This builds an association in the dog's mind that whistle means food!

Most dogs respond very quickly. Once the response is established at meal-times, the exercise will be extended. For example, when the dog is distracted, playing, or even resting in another room, on hearing the whistle being blown, he should immediately run to the source of the sound and be rewarded for doing so. The distance between dog and handler will slowly be increased until the dog is carrying out the procedure from anywhere in the house, or from the garden into the house, before introducing the procedure on a free run.

The socialiser will also develop good behaviour from the dog while he is in the company of other pets and animals. The training centre owns a variety of animals, including dogs, cats, chickens and rabbits. When the socialiser brings the dog to training classes at the centre, time will be spent introducing the dog to other animals to develop a friendly attitude.

The puppy socialiser will be visited regularly by one of the training staff. These checks establish the dog's rate of progress and the training staff are there to train and help the socialiser achieve the dog's full potential as quickly as possible. Unsuitable dogs are weeded out early on, so the socialiser's time can be used more effectively on a more suitable dog. Twenty-seven per cent of dogs are rejected at the socialising stage; they are rarely rejected after this time.

WHO CAN BENEFIT FROM A HEARING DOG?

Hearing loss is experienced by one in seven of the population in the UK, and is measured in decibels at four levels:

- **Mild hearing loss**
  There are 4,645,000 people with a decibel level of between 25-40 per cent loss, roughly 10 per cent of the adult population.

- **Moderate hearing loss**
  There are 3,323,000 people who have a 40-70 per cent hearing loss, making up 7.1 per cent of the adult population.

Candy, the 1,000th selected puppy, with her socialisers, the Routh family.

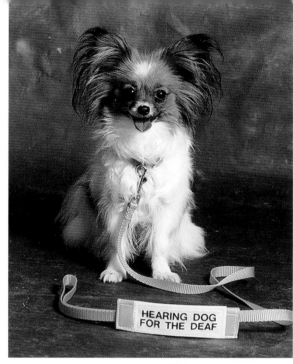

The Papillon is one of the most successful dogs to qualify.

- **Severe hearing loss**
  There are 532,000 who have a 70-90 per cent hearing loss, making up 1.1 per cent of the adult population.

- **Profoundly deaf**
  There are 141,000 people who have at least a 95 per cent hearing loss, making up 0.3 per cent of the adult population.

Hearing Dogs for Deaf People qualified 100 dogs in 1998. Of these dogs, the Labrador and the Papillon were the most successful of the pure-bred dogs to qualify. Labrador crosses and terrier crosses have also proved themselves to be good Hearing Dogs.

ASSESSING AND MATCHING

The trainer has some time to assess the dog during the period of socialisation and, once the dog returns to the centre, he will undergo a two-week assessment. Matching the dog to a recipient will be carried out after the dog has completed his assessment stage.

The dog will be tested for his level of voice response to control commands and sound response. The dog will be taken into the town environment, to see how well he copes with shops, steps, lifts, crowds, noise and children. He will be taken on a bus and a train to ensure he travels well.

How the dog reacts to the constantly changing environment and how easily he is controlled within those situations is an important factor when considering his suitability. The dog's social behaviour is also checked. Social behaviour is defined as 'good manners' (not jumping up at people, not leaping on furniture, etc.) A dog who is attentive, easy to live with, enjoys playing and being groomed, and who is already showing a good response to the squeaker sound, will be accepted for training.

Each dog will be trained to suit a particular recipient's individual requirements, so that matching the right dog to the right owner is important. For example, if a recipient uses public transport regularly, then the dog has to be confident about travelling in this way. If the recipient has children or grandchildren, the dog must be relaxed and happy in the company of children. A recipient with a baby would probably want the dog to alert her to the baby alarm.

Once a prospective owner has been interviewed and accepted, a plan of their home will be used to modify the training house to a similar layout. This familiarises the dog to the routes around the house, furniture positioning and the different sound directions he will experience once at home with the new owner.

CASE HISTORY

CHARLIE TURRELL AND MICKEY

Name: Charlie Turrell.
Hearing Dog: Mickey, a working Cocker Spaniel.
Family: Single.
Occupation/interests: Former civil engineer.

Being partially-sighted, as well as deaf, Charlie finds Mickey's help and companionship invaluable. Courtesy of Pembroke Photography.

Charlie was diagnosed, at the age of 17, to be suffering from Usher Syndrome, a genetically inherited condition which causes deafness from birth and gradual sight loss. Many born deaf with Usher syndrome learn to communicate through the use of British sign language. As their sight becomes more affected, their ability to see sign language or to lip-read becomes increasingly limited, presenting the individual with enormous communication difficulties with the hearing and sighted world. Charlie signs or writes to communicate – though his use of British sign language has a few non-textbook additions.

‘ I have some difficulty communicating with my dog verbally, so I have taught him some hand signals. Running the fingers of my left hand along my right arm, means 'let's go for a walk'. On a walk, I will give him permission to swim if it is a nice day. As soon as I mime the breast stroke, Mickey leaps into the water. If I put my hands together and hold them close to my face, Mickey will go to bed. I pretend to eat to indicate that it is feeding time, and, if I want Mickey to find a toy so we can have a game, I put the first finger of each hand in my mouth and pull my lips wide apart.

"We always had pet dogs when I lived at home. As a family, we particularly like Border Terriers. Bilbo was especially clever. Because my bedroom was at the top of the house, my mother would have to climb the stairs to get me up in the morning, call me for a meal or just to speak with me – shouting was a total waste of time. The same problem existed if I was in the garden or just in another room to the rest of the family. Someone had to make the effort to actually come and get me.

"Mum had to do more than most and it used to drive her mad. She decided to do something practical about the problem, so she trained Bilbo to come and indicate to me that I was wanted. Bilbo would be sent to 'find Charlie'. Once the dog had located me, he would jump up at me to indicate I was wanted, and I would then give him a treat.

Bilbo loved it, he thought it was a great game, and it saved my mother's sanity!

"Mum was so delighted with Bilbo's enthusiasm to learn, she rang Tony Blunt at the Hearing Dogs training centre to ask him to visit us and see if Bilbo could be taught anything else. Mr Blunt was impressed with Bilbo's demonstration, and asked if Bilbo was typical of the breed. We had owned Border Terriers for years and always found them to be confident, intelligent and willing to please, so we felt we could say 'yes'.

"Mum went one step further and purchased a puppy – Bilbo's half-brother – from the breeder. She donated him to Hearing Dogs, so they could see the breed's potential for themselves. The organisation has gone on to use several Border Terriers that have been offered to them through the Border Terrier rescue society.

"Before my eyesight deteriorated, I worked as a civil engineer, specialising in computer graphics for a company based in Epsom, Surrey. When it got to the stage where I could no longer work on the computer, I was made redundant. I decided to move to Chippenham to be nearer my mother. We couldn't live in the same house – we would drive each other mad – but it is nice to know she is just down the road!

"I am a very active person and need plenty to do. So once I had settled in my new home, I decided to attend a four-year accounting course at the local college. I enjoy the company and it keeps the old grey matter ticking over!

"Bilbo died soon after I moved back to Chippenham. I missed the company and security of a dog, so I applied for a Hearing Dog and had to wait for some time. When they did contact me to say they had a suitable dog for me, they offered me a choice of two. The first dog, a Sealyham type, was all white, but with my sight problem, I found it hard to see him. The second dog, Mickey, was a black-and-white Cocker Spaniel, and a totally different character: lively, enthusiastic and visible.

"I saw Mickey in June and went for training in September. It was a long few months. I was allowed to see Mickey once during his training time, so I wouldn't be a total stranger to him. It was hard to walk away, but I knew it wouldn't be long before we would spend a week in training together.

"I arrived at the centre all prepared to stay in one of the purpose-built, self-contained houses. No sooner had I arrived than training began. Mickey was brought from the kennels over to the house and there he stayed for the rest of the week – not only to practise all the training procedures, but to spend time with me to develop a bond between us. It didn't take long, we just seemed to 'click'. Mickey was ideal, bright, affectionate and loved a game as well as a cuddle.

"Our first training task was to get Mickey to make contact with me every time he heard a squeaker. I then had to reward him with a tasty treat. This had to be practised with Mickey in the same room or elsewhere in the house, asleep or engrossed in playing.

"Before, Mickey had been taught to run to his trainer and touch her leg with a paw to alert her to various sounds. Mickey now had to alert me – would he work for me? I need not have worried; Mickey seemed instantly to accept me as his new owner.

"For every sound – other than the smoke alarm – Mickey ran up to me, wherever he was. Once he had gained my attention, I would ask 'what is it?' and open my arms, a signal to the dog to show me. This gesture triggers the dog to lead me to the specific sound. The only sound Mickey did not lead me to was the sound of the smoke alarm. In the event of a real fire, leading me towards it could be dangerous. Instead, when the smoke alarm rang out, Mickey ran to me and then would lie down to indicate clearly it was the smoke alarm.

"The other useful task Mickey learnt was to retrieve. I never realised just how useful this would be. As my sight has deteriorated, I find it difficult to find items that I drop. I have to wear a baseball cap to shade my eyes from the sun or glaring skies, and it frequently gets blown off on a windy day. Mickey is always

Charlie's mother recognised the Border Terrier's skill as a Hearing Dog.

quick to retrieve it. If I drop my keys or money, he will pick them up. I am always dropping pegs when I hang my washing out! But Mickey is constantly ready to help me out.

"We did have one small problem during our first week's training. Mickey was quick to assess that my bed was more comfortable than his! We had three very sleepless nights – every time he jumped up on to the bed, I had to make him get off. The only time Mickey is allowed on the bed is to alert me to the sound of the alarm clock. To be allowed to stay on the bed would affect the desired response – every time the dog moved in the night, I would think it was time to get up. One very disgruntled dog soon realised I wasn't going to let him get away with his attempts to bend the rules.

"During the training week, I was taught how to care for the dog – feeding routine, grooming procedures and how to check Mickey's ears, eyes, feet and pads for problems. I also had to learn how to control him when he is on the lead. Mickey must walk steadily beside me in any situation. He must not pull – firstly, because it would become a bad habit, but also, if he pulls me, it can affect my balance and cause me to fall. He must 'sit' and 'wait' while I shop, and behave calmly in the company of children and other animals. We also have to travel on buses, and I go to London regularly by train, so this needed to be practised.

"Regular free exercise is important to keep Mickey fit and happy. We practised recall every day throughout the week. The dogs are taught to respond to the sound of the whistle if they run further than a short distance away. Two blasts on the whistle bring Mickey racing back to my side; he will either get a titbit or have a big fuss and cuddle for doing so. Mickey loves his free runs. Once a week, Mum brings her dog, Merlin, over and we take both dogs to the local country park. Mickey loves to go swimming, but it isn't always convenient – it may be too cold or I might be going on elsewhere to someone's home, who wouldn't appreciate a wet smelly dog. So I taught him the breast-stroke hand signal. That way he swims when I want him to, not when he feels like it!

"We have regular visits to ensure that Mickey's training transfers successfully to the home and work environment. We go out with the trainer on local routes, which include trips to the shops, college, the doctor's and to the vet. Mickey has to be checked over by the vet every six months. He needs to be regularly wormed, receive an annual booster vaccination and, most importantly, to be weighed. Using food as a reward for the tasks he completes can lead to putting on excess weight, so it is really important that I get him weighed regularly.

"Over a period of 12 weeks, Mickey and I had regular visits from the placement officer, Ann. Even when you go home with the dog after the initial week's training, you don't know if you will qualify and therefore be able to keep the dog at this stage. Every time Ann came, she checked Mickey's sound responses and my response to my dog. All the sounds that I use regularly were practised.

"The front door bell caused some amusement. On one of Ann's visits, she had just arrived and we were sitting chatting about how Mickey and I were getting on when the front door bell rang unexpectedly. Mickey got up, looked to the front door, which has a glass panel in it, saw it was my mother and lay down again. We roared with laughter, his whole body language said "She's got a key and

Mickey loves the great outdoors.

can let herself in." Mickey also got a little over-enthusiastic with my mother's mobile phone – he only had to see it and he was telling me it was ringing, whether it was or not!

"Ann was there to help us through any early teething problems. She checked Mickey's social behaviour around the house and leash behaviour out on a walk. We walked the route to the college and went in to check Mickey's reaction to the steps, lifts and slippery floors he was going to encounter regularly in this building. We also had to have the chance to do a fire practice and ensure Mickey responded to the new sound of the college fire alarm.

"Mickey became very reliable during our first three months together. The fire alarm test at the college was executed perfectly: Mickey pawed at my legs and instantly lay on the floor in front of me. I looked to Ann. Had we passed the important test? She smiled and signed to me that she was delighted with our standard of work and we would be qualifying. This meant that Mickey would be presented with his official yellow jacket. It's like passing your driving test – one of those momentous occasions.

"Mickey now provides me with a degree of independence that for a deaf and partially sighted person is hard to achieve. He is always there for me, and is definitely my best mate! **'**

TRAINING A HEARING DOG

The daily training regime consists of a combination of obedience and social behaviour, sound work and training the dog in a busy environment. Basic obedience commands are taught to the dog. As the profoundly deaf can find the achievement of clear speech difficult, the dogs are taught to respond to hand signals for the 'sit', and 'down' command. The dog is taught to 'come' to the sound of a whistle and also to walk to heel. When the dog is being taught to lead the trainer to the source of the sound, a hand signal for 'what is it?' is used, where the handler opens his arms.

HAND SIGNALS
- The hand signal for 'sit' is a flat hand being raised.
- The hand signal for 'down' is the hand pointing to the ground/floor.

Davey Nauth gives the hand-signal for 'What is it?', as Hearing Dog Carlton alerts him to the phone.

- The hand signal for 'down' can also be used to get the dog to settle in his bed or by the side of the handler.
- The hand signal for 'what is it?' is an open hand gesture.

A good retrieve response is developed. This is useful to the owner if they want the dog to pick up any dropped items, but it also helps to consolidate a good recall response.

The dog has already experienced the sound of the squeaker with the socialiser. Once the dog is responding and touching the trainer every time he hears the squeaker, training can progress. The way the dog is encouraged to touch the trainer depends on the individual dog, his size and enthusiasm. A large dog would be taught an appropriate touch signal. Too much physical contact could lead to rough behaviour.

SOUND TRAINING

The first sound the dog is taught to respond to is the alarm clock. On hearing the alarm, the dog has to sit or stand by the bed and touch the trainer by pawing. Smaller dogs are encouraged to jump on the bed to alert the trainer to the sound.

The second stage of training requires the dog to touch and then lead the trainer to the sound. The new sound could be the telephone or a front door bell. The distance between the trainer and the source of the sound will initially be small. As the dog learns, so the distance will be gradually increased. In the early stages of training, the dog is taught this response with the use of plenty of vocal encouragement and physical praise as well as a treat, given by the trainer on arriving at the source of the sound. For example, if the dog is leading the trainer to the telephone, the treat would be placed underneath the telephone.

As the dog's understanding of the task develops and the response becomes more automatic, the trainer may have to reduce the amount of vocal encouragement that is given the dog. A future owner may not be able to communicate with the dog clearly, so it is important that the dog does not rely totally on this type of reward. Physical praise and food are the main methods of reward.

As the dog progresses, different sounds are introduced. He will be taught to respond to the telephone, front door bell, baby alarm if required and a timer used for cooking. Recipients are advised not to use the timer on the cooker; use of a separate timer reduces any risk of the dog jumping at the cooker whilst it is in use to alert the owner to the sound.

The smoke or fire alarm is the last sound response to be taught. It requires a different reaction from the dog. It is taught at the end of training once the dog has an established reaction to all the other introduced sounds. On hearing the smoke or fire alarm, the dog must touch the owner to alert them. Once the dog has the attention of the trainer, the trainer will ask and signal 'what is it?'. The dog must not lead to the sound, he must lie down in front of the trainer. This action indicates that this is the smoke or fire alarm and caution is required.

During training, it is important to ensure that the trainer is not giving the dog any subtle indicators, such as eye movement, body language or facial expressions that the dog could pick up and respond to rather than the sound itself. Dogs can quickly learn to anticipate the sounds if the trainer inadvertently gives them a signal. To ensure this does not happen, the trainer will bury themselves under the bedcovers when teaching the morning alarm, put on eye shades if sitting,

The Hearing Dog is taught to touch the trainer and lead her to the sound.

and perhaps use ear defenders while carrying out a household task during sound practice.

Good social behaviour and leash work will be taught in a variety of situations. The trainer will use the facilities at the training centre as well as taking the dog into the local town. Trips to town on market day provide a variety of distractions including noise and rubbish. Visits to cafes and libraries are undertaken to develop desirable behaviour. The dog is expected to lie down and wait calmly while the owner shops or visits public buildings. The dog must not pull on the lead, or jump up at people he meets. He must not be excessively distracted by other dogs or children, and he must ignore litter on the pavement.

TRAINING THE RECIPIENT

Each applicant is assessed on their own ability and must have a severe or profound hearing loss. It has to be evident to the Deaf Liaison Officer, who interviews the applicant at home, that they have a genuine need for a dog to assist them regularly at home or at their place of work. Generally this would be someone who lives alone or spends a large part of the day on their own or someone who lives with another disabled or deaf person. If the applicant works, agreement has to be sought from the employer to allow the dog to accompany the recipient to work.

The applicant must also want and enjoy the companionship a dog can offer and accept all the responsibilities of dog ownership. There should be no other pet living in the house, although a case may be made if the pet is elderly. The distraction of another pet could affect the dog's working ability.

During training, the recipient will live in one of the training houses for a week. The dog lives with the recipient from the moment they arrive at the centre. This helps to establish a fast relationship between dog and new owner. It is important that the dog switches allegiance from the trainer to the deaf owner as quickly as possible.

Each day spent at the training centre will include two sound sessions, and lead, obedience and social behaviour practice, including recall. The recipient will also be taught about grooming, feeding, health-care, and the responsibilities of owning a dog – everything from how to bath the

dog, to the importance of picking up if he relieves himself in a public area. The first week at the centre and at home are crucial to the new team's success. It requires a lot of time, concentration and effort on the part of everyone concerned.

When the recipient first returns home with their dog, they will be given a few days to settle into their new environment and routine. The dog will not be expected to work until he has become confident in his new surroundings. The following week, the placement officer will visit and the new partnership will practise the four important aspects of successfully owning a Hearing Dog: sound response, good social behaviour, lead behaviour and general obedience. It usually takes three days of support and encouragement before the recipient is left to continue to practise the procedures on their own. The recipient has to complete a daily written report on their progress

It takes time for trainers to build a close rapport with a Hearing Dog.

and the placement officer returns three weeks later to check on progress and help sort out any teething problems.

TRAINING STAFF

It takes six months to develop the trainer's dog handling skills, after which time there is a practical and written examination. As part of their training, they have to learn at least stage one of the British sign language course, and, if they want to become a placement officer, they have to pass stage two.

The trainee is allocated to an experienced member of staff to learn the different methods and approaches to training. Each trainer usually has four or five dogs in training at any one time. Every dog is different, so a flexible approach to training is essential. Once the dog has been trained, he is handed over to the placement officer for training with the new owner.

The placement officer trains the owner on a one-to-one basis at the centre and then visits the recipient regularly over a period of three months to establish good routines and practices before the owner and the dog are allowed to qualify. The placement officer spends a lot of time away from home. This is not the sort of job for someone who does not like staying away!

The approach and attitude of the placement officer is the key to success. They need to be able to motivate, direct, and, in some cases, control the recipient and the dog. Encouragement and support in the early days are essential if the team is to qualify.

CASE HISTORY

HUMPHRY BRIERLEY AND TED

Name: Humphry Brierley.
Hearing Dog: Ted, a Norwegian Buhund.
Family: Married with two children.
Occupation/interests: Former Officer Cadet at Sandhurst.

Humphry says Ted is his best friend, and it looks as if this sentiment is mutual.

'While serving as an Officer Cadet at Sandhurst Military College, I was involved in an artillery accident which damaged my hearing. I suffered a 75 per cent hearing loss and was discharged from the Army. Being deaf and trying to continue to work was a frustrating and demoralising experience. Communication is always the main problem and the resulting discrimination presented many obstacles.

"I rely 100 per cent on lip-reading. In a conversation on a one-to-one basis, usually I can get away with only having to guess 20 per cent of the words said. In a multiple conversation, though, I will probably lose 80 per cent of the words and most likely not get the context of the conversation at all. This would often make me very angry or even depressed.

"In 1994, I gave up work, as communicating with people became more and more difficult, and I completely lost the small amount of confidence I had. I was fearful of people coming up behind me or being surprised by someone's unexpected presence. I found staying at home an easier option.

"I became a recluse – that way I wouldn't have to tell anyone that I was deaf. I sat in a chair all day and would read or sleep the day away. That way, I could shut the world out.

"My wife, Sue, made the initial application for a Hearing Dog in 1994. She decided something had to be done to restore my confidence, and thought perhaps a dog could help. She had the support of my hearing therapist, who also thought it was a good idea – anything was worth a try!

"My Hearing Dog Ted is a pedigree Norwegian Buhund. The breeder had kept Ted as a prospective show dog and stud dog. Unfortunately, after genetic testing, he was found to be a carrier of the cataract gene, but not a sufferer himself. To control this hereditary eye problem, which Ted could pass on to any progeny, it was decided to neuter him. This also meant he could not be a show dog, so his owner gave him to Hearing Dogs, and for this I shall be ever-grateful.

"I had to wait for a year to be called for training, which is about the average waiting time. In May 1995, we were trained together. Slowly, with Ted's support, my life has changed. Now I have to go out, as Ted needs his daily exercise, and I always enjoyed

Ted alerts Humphry to a variety of sounds, including the Minicom and the doorbell.

Lie-ins are a thing of the past thanks to Ted's amazing sense of time-keeping.

walking in the past. Now I am back in the habit. We meet other regular walkers and friends, and I even go to the pub. As my confidence in my ability to communicate has increased, I now go out more, visiting different places and shopping. I have even become a speaker for Hearing Dogs!

"Ted, in his yellow jacket, helps to identify to the public that I am deaf. People make a greater effort to interact with me and they will look at me, which helps with the lip-reading. Ted attracts a lot of attention when we are out; he is such an attractive little dog, complete strangers stop and talk to us. It is good therapy for Ted's ego and gives me more opportunity to practise my lip-reading skills.

"Ted goes about the routine jobs he was trained to do very efficiently. He responds to the door bell, telephone and the cooker. He is also quick to respond to new sounds that he thinks he should alert me to. A few months ago, my car broke down. Whilst it was being repaired, the garage loaned me another car – it was rather a swish model, giving a very smooth silent ride. I was a bit terrified of it as, in my old car, I could feel by the vibration when I needed to change gear, but this car was a different matter. Nevertheless Ted and I had shopping to do, so we had to use it. With Ted sitting on the front seat beside me, off we went.

"Within a matter of seconds, we had only travelled a few hundred yards when Ted

started to touch me to indicate there was a noise he thought I should know about. Obviously, he couldn't take me to it, so I pulled up, got out and walked around the car. I could see no obvious signs of anything wrong. But Ted was insistent there was a noise. Getting back into the car, I noticed a small flashing light on the dashboard that I had not seen before. On asking at the garage, I was told that, not only did it flash, but the petrol warning light also bleeped a warning sound to alert the driver. Good old Ted, he was right again!

"Ted has a cheeky sense of humour. He wakes me when the alarm clock goes off by jumping on me. On the days I don't set the clock, such as weekends and holidays, good old Ted still wakes me at the same time, almost to the minute. Ted enthusiastically tramples me, as if to say, "You silly old fool, you have forgotten to set the clock again!"

"One of Ted's most important roles is to let me know if the smoke alarm goes off; for this, he gets a special treat. It is my role to get the breakfast every morning, while Sue gets ready for work. I put the bread in the toaster and, as soon as the smell of toast is in the air, Ted comes rushing into the kitchen and sits waiting for the smoke alarm to go off, as I invariably burn the toast!

"During the early days of our partnership, Ted was quick to assess me and react to my lack of confidence or even fear in certain

Ted has helped Humphry to interact with others, putting an end to his reclusive isolation.

situations. I suffer from a lack of balance and rely on visual compensation to counteract feelings of vertigo and maintain my balance. Ted and I were out shopping one day, and, turning the corner at the end of the high street, I was faced directly into bright sunlight. I lost sight of my route for a moment and therefore lost my balance and fell badly, hurting myself. I had inadvertently dropped Ted's lead. Reacting immediately, he ran to the nearest group of people and got their much-needed help.

"I have so many stories about life with Ted – he is such a wonderful dog. He is an invaluable companion, particularly because I am retired, but my wife still works long hours as a nurse, so I am on my own a lot. It is at this time in my silent world that I need Ted so much. He tells me everything that is going on around us. He is my best friend. '

3 DOGS FOR THE DISABLED

Having to rely on other people to help you do simple tasks is frustrating and demoralising. Even when the help comes from a family member or a good friend, coping with this dependence is no less difficult. There is little choice of how or when to do what you want. Imagine, then, how a trained dog can transform the life of someone in this position. At last, the decisions most adults take for granted can be made again: when to go to bed, when to go shopping, when to go out just for the sake of it because it's a sunny day. Imagine no telephone calls to ask friends for help, just a quiet word to a loving companion and off you go!

To those who have been deprived of it, independence is a greatly treasured commodity

Dogs for the Disabled do not simply offer love and companionship, they also allow their owners to lead independent lives.

and it can be returned by the loving loyalty of a well-trained dog.

HISTORY OF THE DOG FOR THE DISABLED

The positive effect that animals can have on patients is mentioned in literature dating back to the 18th century. It was trialed at the York Retreat, a psychiatric unit that recognised the benefits and encouraged the patients to care for rabbits and poultry as part of their rehabilitation programme. It is not until the last 20 years that scientific studies began to examine the relationship between animals and humans and the practical help this relationship obviously provides.

There are now many organisations in the USA and Europe that train dogs to assist disabled people. Canine Companions for Independence in Santa Rosa, California, is one such organisation. It has now been training dogs for more than 22 years. Its production programme is divided into three categories: service dogs, hearing dogs and social dogs. Many of the overseas schools have this type of combined training programme. Suitable dogs, once assessed, can then be trained in the skill most suited to the temperament of the individual. The Labrador and Golden Retriever are used extensively as service dogs – or assistance dogs, as they are also known.

In the UK, Dogs for the Disabled is a growing organisation set up in 1986 by Francis Hay, who was herself severely affected by bone cancer. She was also a dog lover, who found that her own pet dog, Kim, could be trained to carry out tasks that she was finding increasingly difficult. Opening and closing doors, activating light switches, picking up dropped items and collecting the milk basket, the newspaper and the post are just some of the tasks Kim learned.

There are numerous assistance dog charities around the world.

Aware of how much her own dog helped her, Francis recognised that this was something that many other people in similar circumstances could benefit from. A determined lady, she motivated a small group of like-minded family and friends, and, from small beginnings, the charity grew. Sadly, Francis died in 1990, but the effort she put into this passionate belief was continued by friends and family, enabling Dogs for the Disabled to become a registered charity in 1988.

In the early days, Dogs for the Disabled developed with the support and co-operation of the Guide Dogs for the Blind Association, which provided some of its trainee dogs and experienced training staff. Often, adult dogs rejected from the Guide Dog training programme, made good dogs for disabled people. However, a new national training centre has now been purchased to deal with the growing demand for the disabled Dog.

The Dogs for the Disabled mission statement identifies the charity's main aims. It is dedicated to enhancing the independence, security and companionship available to people with disabilities by:

• Identifying the practical needs of individual people with disabilities.
• Training dogs to perform practical tasks to meet those individual needs.
• Creating and supporting working partnerships between assistance dogs and people with disabilities.

CASE HISTORY

CAROL FLETCHER AND TARN

Name: Carol Fletcher.
Dog for the Disabled: Tarn, a Border Collie.
Family: Married, with a baby.
Occupation/interests: The music business.

When Carol drew up the guest list for her wedding, there was one name that was certain to be there: Dog for the Disabled, Tarn, a six-year-old Border Collie. He had become so much a part of Carol's life over the past four years that arriving at the church without such a good friend in attendance was unthinkable.

Proudly taking up his position alongside the bridesmaids and pageboys, Tarn's presence completed a perfect day, which only a few years ago, would have been impossible for the bride to imagine.

' Tarn has given me back my life. He has made such a difference. You can't put a measure on the confidence and companionship I get from him.

"Fourteen years ago, I suffered a brain haemorrhage. In time, and with help, my speech returned, but I remained permanently paralysed down one side of my body, making walking extremely difficult. Even the simplest everyday tasks are a struggle. Hobbies, activities, a job, going out with friends – the kind of lifestyle most people in their early twenties take for granted – became further and further beyond reach.

"I spent a lot of time at home, because getting out was so hard. You begin to feel so lonely and, being so dependent on other people, your confidence soon starts to be sapped. Then it becomes a downward spiral.

"The turning point came when a friend who had a Guide Dog told me about the organisation, Dogs for the Disabled. Having enjoyed owning a dog in the past, I needed no persuasion to apply. I went on the waiting list. It can take a while, as they try to match the dog to the owner and the disability. Though the basic training is the same for all, once a possible match has been decided, the dogs are then trained with that particular person in mind, according to the tasks they will need to do.

"I don't need to be helped out of my wheelchair, for example, but those people that do, need a solid, steady type of dog that can support the person as they manoeuvre. Being a Border Collie, Tarn is quite lively and quick thinking, so he wouldn't suit that type of

Carol has shared so much of her life with Tarn, that it was unthinkable that he wouldn't be there for her big day.

Carol and Tarn, a perfect duo.

work; but he is ideal for me.

"The trainee dogs come from various sources. Many of them trained to become Guide Dogs, but were not suitable for one reason or another. Tarn was actually donated to the organisation as an adult dog, as his breeder specifically wanted him to become a Dog for the Disabled.

"Tarn's preliminary training taught him obedience, social behaviour and hygiene discipline (relieving on command). He was also taught to walk on the left-hand side of the wheelchair, because I am unable to use my right-hand side.

"When Tarn and I first met for our fortnight's intensive training together, Tarn already knew as much about household chores as most self-respecting housekeepers: loading and unloading the washing machine, tidying away, retrieving the post and fetching a ringing mobile phone adapted to enable the

dog to pick it up. He opened and closed doors, switched on the light, carried the shopping basket – Tarn was the kind of domestic help anyone would like to employ!

"For two weeks, you spend every waking moment with your dog. You carry out your daily routine, shopping, going to the doctors and all the other things you would normally do. The instructor is there to encourage, help, advise and redirect if things go a bit wrong, but on the whole, you just get on with it.

"The bond between the two of us was immediate. I didn't have to worry about it taking time for us to gel, as we got on well right from the start.

"When Tarn first arrived home, he was so used to walking beside a wheelchair that when my young niece visited and was scooting around on her tricycle, there was Tarn trotting steadily along by her side, following every turn – he has to be looking after someone all of the time.

"For Tarn, simply being with you is all-important. This is an essential characteristic for any assistance dog, and is a particular quality of the Border Collie which makes it especially suited to the carer's role.

"Their love of companionship, I believe, is their most important quality. The Border Collie is so faithful and loyal, coupled with their intelligence, it makes them very special. My particular dog absolutely loves everyone, especially children – and yet he knows he is there for me. Whatever else is going on, he watches every move I make. Even if I go out of the room, I swear he can see through doors! His eyes follow me everywhere. It is more than just obedience – it is a strong bond.

"Tarn is definitely a 'people dog'. It is in his nature to be a carer. We went away and left him with friends who have children. Apparently, he spent the whole time rounding up the children, checking where each one was and what they were up to.

"The Border Collie seems to have an innate need to be useful and gain the all-important approval of his owner. Tarn is never happier then when being asked to perform a task. As a Dog for the Disabled, he could hardly have better job satisfaction. He willingly gets the post, empties the washing machine and picks up anything I drop.

"My husband and I are now proud parents to 16-month-old Katie. Her arrival brought about a whole new range of tasks. Tarn will fetch nappies (clean ones), pots of cream, talcum powder and toys thrown out of the pram. And, of course, the washing machine seems to be in constant use.

"Katie provided Tarn with more to do, just the sort of lifestyle a Border Collie likes. But now Katie is mobile, she is fascinated by Tarn and the things he does. It has become a race between them – who can get to the post first? It is so funny watching Katie copy the dog.

"Wherever I go, Tarn goes, too. As a singer, I get invited to perform at weddings and parties. Tarn comes to most of my gigs, and lies there listening to the music. I'm not sure what he thinks of it, but he hasn't complained yet.

"I met my husband indirectly through the music business – he sold me my first microphone. He is very fond of Tarn and is always willing to take him for a walk. He loves it when Tarn gets his slippers! We run our own business now, hiring out sound equipment. I work part-time, trying to keep on top of the office work. Tarn is as helpful at work as he is at home. I am always dropping pens, files or order forms, so he is such a great help when it comes to keeping the office in order. Perhaps I could train him to do the filing as well!

"Tarn is always good company and is very sensitive to my moods. On the rare occasions that I have cried, he has been so concerned for me, it was moving. When I received a phone call telling me my grandmother had died, I must have sounded upset: although he did not understand the conversation, there he was, trying to climb on top of me, desperately trying to comfort me. It was quite strange – he clearly knew that something was not right and he wanted to make it better.

"Tarn means so much to me, I cannot put it into words. Remembering all the details of our life together is difficult, because to Tarn and I, it is everyday life. To every-one else, he is amazing. **'**

The Golden Retriever has proved to be a popular and successful breed in the training programme.

SOURCE OF SUPPLY

At present, any dog rejected from the Guide Dog training programme, that is considered to have some potential as a working dog, will then be offered to Dogs for the Disabled to train. Many dogs that have proved unsuitable to be a Guide Dog have qualified as a dog for a disabled person.

The organisation also accepts puppies offered to them – Labradors, Golden Retrievers, first crosses of these breeds and some Border Collies. A few other breeds have been tried, with some success. The following list shows the breeds that qualified for Dogs for the Disabled in 1998. The 31 new teams bring the total number of working teams to 127:

> 9 Golden Retrievers
> 8 Labrador Retrievers
> 3 Labrador crosses
> 2 Golden Retriever-collie crosses
> 2 Standard Poodles
> 1 Golden Retriever-Labrador cross
> 1 Labrador-collie cross
> 1 Leonberger
> 1 German Shepherd Dog
> 1 Crossbreed
> 1 Finnish Lapphund
> 1 Springer Spaniel

Dogs for the Disabled will often purchase puppies from breeders who have used a Guide Dog stud dog, and those that are 50 per cent Guide Dog-bred often prove to be more successful. The Guide Dog breeding programme has established Labrador and Golden Retriever lines that have been selectively bred to produce dogs with a desirable working temperament that are as free as possible from the common health problems associated with these breeds.

PUPPY-WALKING

Puppies' early training is very similar to that of Guide Dogs' puppy-walked stock. They are placed in homes for their first 14 months. As with Guide Dog puppies, early socialisation and education are crucial to the dog's success.

Puppies are walked by volunteer members of the public, getting the puppy used to all the sights

Puppy-walkers are essential to the organisation's success.

and sounds of everyday life, such as busy town centres, buses, train rides and shopping precincts. The puppies are taught the basic obedience responses, good leash behaviour, and how to behave socially at home, when visiting or at public functions. It is important to be able to take a working dog anywhere, knowing he will be the model of good behaviour because it has been well socialised right from the start.

In addition, the puppy will be taught how to retrieve. The desire to retrieve is an essential element to the dog's work as a Dog for the Disabled. The pup will be encouraged to pick up all sorts of articles, soft and hard, as well as different textures, including plastic, rubber and metal. Dogs can be reluctant to pick up metal objects because of the metallic taste and because they can be difficult to grip. Other textures can encourage the dog to mouth or chew the object. Early introduction to picking up various items all helps later on during the formal training programme.

Because the dog may be expected to walk beside a wheelchair later in life as a working dog, the puppy is introduced to walking beside a pram, pushchair, shopping trolley or bicycle. Puppy-walkers are encouraged to take the puppy to nursing homes and clinics where wheelchairs are common. The puppy needs to interact with people who use wheelchairs, and such people are usually only too pleased to speak to or have a cuddle with a puppy. This helps to build up a pleasant association with what the puppy sees as an unusually large obstacle. Formal wheelchair training is carried out once the dog returns to the training centre.

Dogs for the Disabled will also accept adult dogs offered to them for training. Pet dogs who need rehoming may be suitable to train. The charity has also trained a few dogs that came in from rescue centres. The basic requirement is that the dog is sound and confident in a busy environment, ignores noisy traffic, and is friendly and confident with people and other animals. The potential trainee needs to show an interest in retrieving and be fit and healthy. This type of dog will require more time in training to condition him to the town environment and perhaps to undo previously learned habits, such as getting on the furniture or stealing. But the effort is usually rewarded and the dog will qualify even if it takes a little longer to do so.

WHO CAN BENEFIT FROM A DOG?

Dogs for the Disabled can help many people with a range of disabilities. There are 19,050 registered disabled people in England, and this figure does not include people on the blind register.

Dogs for the Disabled have found five health conditions that are common in those applying for a dog: strokes, multiple sclerosis, spina bifida, cerebral palsy, and spinal injuries.

Each applicant is individually interviewed and assessed. If the applicant is suitable, and would benefit from owning a dog, they are placed on a waiting list until a suitable dog is found.

Once the applicant has been successfully matched with a suitable dog, the partnership undergoes an intensive two-week training programme. Depending on the applicant's personal circumstances and degree of disability, training may

Adult dogs from pet homes or rescue centres are sometimes suitable as Dogs for the Disabled.

be completed at home (domiciliary training) or on a residential course. The training centre must be equipped to cope with a variety of disabilities. In a lot of cases, it is easier for all concerned that training takes place at the recipient's home, where the dog can get used to any specific equipment such as stair-lifts, ramps, hoists, reduced-height work-surfaces etc. Some recipients also need a daily visit from home carers.

Basic training takes two weeks. If the applicant has been trained at the training centre, it will be followed with a two-week home placement period. The instructor will visit on a daily basis to ensure a smooth transition of the dog's work to the home environment and areas visited locally on a regular basis.

During training, dog handling skills have to be taught to the new owner, such as basic obedience. This is followed by lead work and control commands. A disabled owner is usually very proficient at negotiating local routes, either in a wheelchair or on crutches. The additional responsibility of controlling a dog at their side takes time and practice in a variety of situations.

The dog may find it difficult to transfer his affections from his trainer to his new owner.

One of the hardest parts of training is the transition of the dog from working for the instructor to working for the new owner. The dog is obviously attached to the instructor, and the owner has to work hard to win the dog's loyalty.

Timing of praise and when to reward are other skills that have to be learned. A lot of clients have never owned a dog before, so they have to be taught how to use vocal intonation, body language and facial expressions correctly. The owner has to practise training exercises to learn the subtleties of effective handling. Learning just how much they can affect the dog's motivation has to be explained and experienced to see the benefits of getting it right.

Obviously, there will be highs and lows during training, and it is the job of the instructor to be able to motivate the client. Everyone learns at a different rate and requires a training process that is individual in style and skill. Encouragement, direction and motivation are teaching skills the instructor has to implement throughout the client's training. No two people or dogs respond in the same way – a flexible approach is essential!

Individual training will be developed during this time. The instructor will continue to work with the partnership until he or she is satisfied with the standard achieved. The partnership will not qualify until this stage is reached. The instructor will only withdraw support once the team are ready to go it alone!

On qualification, the dog receives his official yellow jacket. The new partners have their photograph taken, and a copy of this is given to the puppy-walker or sponsor, in recognition of their efforts and their support of the organisation.

AFTER-CARE

Routine after-care visits are an important part of the work done by the organisation. It is essential to maintain contact with the recipients and their dogs, and regular visits are made to ensure all is well. Help and advice are always available. The partnership will receive a routine after-care visit every six months, although additional visits will be made if necessary.

This may occur if the owner's circumstances or needs change. Some dogs and their owners may need a refresher course – perhaps if the owner has had a long-term stay in hospital, resulting in the dog not being worked for a while. As with any learned behaviour, lack of practice affects the standard of work. Most dogs are quick to re-establish routines and tasks with a short period of refresher training.

CASE HISTORY

NORMA CAIL AND TARA

Name: Norma Cail.
Dog for the Disabled: Tara, a Finnish Lapphund.
Family: Single.
Occupation/interests: Script editor.

While the Finnish Lapphund was originally bred to herd reindeer in Lapland, it is a talent that is rarely needed in Dorset. But the working ability of this breed has been channelled into something completely different and very useful. Tara the Finnish Lapphund has been trained by Dogs for the Disabled to be a working companion for Norma Cail.

'Ten years ago, I suffered a series of strokes, which left me severely disabled, to such an extent that I lived the next six years of my life in a nursing home. During this time, I battled to regain my speech and some of the use in my left arm. I still do not have any use of my left leg. Life in the nursing home took its toll. I was cared for admirably by the staff; my speech and mobility improved, but I became very introverted. I rarely went out to shop or visit old friends, I just kept myself very much to myself.

**Tara, a Finnish Lapphund – a rare breed with a rare talent.
Courtesy of Olan Mills.**

"I felt that life in the home had slowly taken my independence away. I was ready for a change, but suffered from low self-esteem and a lack of confidence. I felt completely incapable of looking after myself. I had been a good cook but I was convinced I couldn't even do that now.

"A new social worker visited me and was a real driving force. She told me, 'Leave it to me, I'll find you a warden-assisted flat. But what you really need is a Dog for the Disabled.'

"Although I was very much a dog lover, I had to think long and hard about applying for a dog. I had settled well into my new flat, I discovered that I could cook and started to enjoy a degree of independence. But I did still rely on an army of home-carers to help me with the housework and, most importantly, to help me into and out of bed. It was this procedure that convinced me that a dog could be just what I needed. The carers were great, and I could obviously not have managed without them. But I dreamt of the day when I could go to bed when I wanted to, rather than at the time the home-carers turned up. Most nights, it was about 9 o'clock, but sometimes it could be earlier.

"To be able to manage on my own, I needed an expensive piece of equipment to get me in and out of bed, plus an extra pair of hands! I was trained with my dog at home – 'domiciliary training' they call it. When Tara arrived, I was determined to stay detached from this dog. I had already suffered a disappointment six months earlier when I had been matched to a dog and had started to train with it, but sadly the local council refused me permission to keep it. At that time, there was a rule that no dogs were allowed in warden-assisted housing developments.

"This second attempt could have been another disappointment. Would the council allow the dog to stay? But more importantly, would I be successful in completing the training course?

"When Caroline, my trainer, pulled up in the car outside the flat, the first thing I noticed was a bushy tail that stuck straight up in the air. It was wagging furiously and my heart melted. I told myself strictly to keep calm and not to get carried away.

"Tara rushed in, straight past me and ran around checking every nook and cranny. Having completed her investigation, she lay down at my feet, on her back with her legs in the air. I was instantly convinced that this funny little character was the dog for me.

"Formal training took three weeks. I found it hard to master timing the basic commands and giving encouragement and praise. Getting the correct intonation in my affected voice was difficult but as with any learning process, practice makes perfect. With the help and support of our trainer, the working relationship between me and Tara grew.

"Tara had some complicated tasks to learn – most importantly, she had to help me get undressed and into bed before Caroline was satisfied that she could withdraw her support. These were the most difficult aspects of day-to-day living. Getting undressed, ably assisted by Tara, is now less of a challenge. Tara enthusiastically pulls off my elasticated clothing, and half-way through the procedure she trots off to the bathroom and fetches my nightie from the side of the bath. Tara knows that she always gets a reward for this. She places the nightie on my lap, takes her reward and returns to the task of pulling my socks off.

"Because I am not quite ready for the nightie, I place it on the back of my wheelchair. With one sock off, Tara goes and fetches the nightie from the back of the wheelchair for yet another treat. Second sock off and, yes, you have guessed it, Tara presents me with my nightie for the third time. She makes me laugh out loud – she knows I will reward her good behaviour even though the whole procedure has become a bit of game!

"Getting into bed was the next specialist task Tara had to learn. To one side of the bed is an electric leg-raiser, this lifts my legs to the same height as the bed. I then hook a leather strap around my ankles and Tara pulls them one at a time across the bed into a comfortable position.

Tara helps in all areas of Norma's life.
Courtesy of *Daily Echo*, Bournemouth

"In the early days of training, one major problem soon became apparent. As Tara pulled the heavy dead weight of my left leg, she was inclined to trample, scratch and bruise my good right leg. So a new task had to be introduced. Tara was encouraged to pull a cover over my right leg to completely protect it, before pulling the left leg into position. She picked up the new routine in no time – she's a real star!

"Tara is so quick to help me. Once I'm straightened up in bed, the best way I can describe myself is something similar to a beached whale. I am inclined to get stuck in that one position, especially if my pillows slip to one side or on to the floor. Because I am so immobile, I get stranded on my back. But my wonderful little dog, Tara, comes to my rescue. If asked to pull, she will enthusiastically tug at the pillows, getting them back into position for me to sort myself out. She will even pick the pillows up off the floor and return them to my bed. Once she has completed the task, we usually have a big cuddle, then I give her one of her favourite treats and, with her tail wagging, she hops off my bed and settles in her own bed for a well-deserved nap.

"Once in bed, I used to have to accept the fact that, if I had forgotten to put an item I might need by the bed, I would have to do without. Now I have Tara, who is always keen to fetch anything on request. She doesn't always get the right item first time, but that's half the fun of the game. I'm convinced Tara gets it wrong deliberately – anything for an extra treat.

"The first time Tara was left with me overnight, she went to bed after her tasks and I quickly dropped off to sleep. Waking with a start in the middle of the night, I lay there listening for Tara breathing, but I couldn't hear a thing. The more I listened, the quieter it all seemed. I began to panic. Had the dog died? I called out, 'Tara, come, come', and, to my great relief, Tara trotted across to me, wagging her tail, looking a lot more bright-eyed and bushy-tailed than I felt. I told her I was sorry, and, after a big hug and cuddle, I sent her back to her bed, but I lay awake for some time, listening to her breathing.

"Tara has given me the gift of independence. I am far more confident now. I recently took my driving test and passed, so Tara and I are really mobile. I also sing in the church choir and play the keyboard. Wherever I go, Tara comes too. We are off to Crufts Dog Show soon, where we have been asked to spend some time on the Dogs for the Disabled stand. What I'm really looking forward to is seeing some other Finnish Lapphunds. There are only about 120 in the country, which classifies them as a rare breed – and I'm lucky enough to have one!

"We have made so many new friends together. Instead of dashing to the shops once a week, we now go three times week. A trip that would take me about an hour, now takes twice as long – so many people talk to us or stop to admire Tara. I always explain how Tara helps me.

"Our most recent escapade was after returning home late one evening after a day out. Getting from the car into my wheelchair is a complicated operation that takes time. Having got myself into the chair, I locked the car and headed for the flat. In my haste to get indoors, the wheelchair clipped the kerb and tipped over, depositing me unceremoniously on to the pavement. I was extremely shaken and knew that I couldn't get back into my chair without assistance. So I encouraged Tara to "Speak" on command. Tara kept on barking until another resident came out to see what all the fuss was about.

"The neighbour found me stranded and cold on the pavement, and quickly organised the help I needed. Tara again had proved invaluable to me. Mind you, her bark is not one you could ignore. It is the most terrible high-pitched yap. I was thankful when someone did come and I could tell Tara to stop!

"Dogs for the Disabled has given me so much more than an assistance dog, they have given me a delightful companion and a purpose to my life. I once relied on two carers that had to come every day, now I rarely need them!

"I spend a lot of my free time giving talks to schools and groups, to spread the news of the good work that a Dog for the Disabled can do. I recently gave a talk to a group and explained that I had little strength and grip in my hands and how Tara will pick up anything that I may drop. Tara was lying beside my wheelchair, apparently sound asleep. A lady in the audience dropped her pen and Tara promptly shot forward, picked up the pen and gave it to me. The audience laughed in amazement. As I said to them: 'Well, how else do you think I get all my pens?'

TRAINING A DOG FOR THE DISABLED

Much of the training is carried out in a specially adapted room, which includes all sorts of training aids: a washing machine for dogs to practise putting laundry in and pulling it out, various telephones with handles attached to enable the dog to grip them, small milk crates, pens, purses, tins, baskets and bags. Articles of different textures are all used to help the dog to learn confidently how to pick up anything that may be dropped by his future owner.

Doors have rope tied to the handles. Instructors teach the dog to pull the rope attached to the handle to open the door. The switches for the wall-lights carry the marks where so many dogs have jumped up when learning to operate the switch.

Each dog will be in training for about six months. On arrival at a training centre, the puppy-walked stock will receive a health-check and undergo a period of assessment. Temperament, willingness, soundness and the standard of previously learned skills are all assessed and recorded. The dog will then be allocated to an instructor for basic training to begin.

Adult stock that has been donated to the organisation will undergo a longer period of assessment, usually lasting one month. It is important to undergo a thorough testing period, ensuring the dog is of sound temperament. He will be tested in as many different situations and environments as possible, before being accepted for training.

Each dog will have a short training session two or three times a day, usually lasting 30 minutes at a time. These will include basic obedience, improving social behaviour and the introduction of basic task work.

Initially, the dogs are taught to retrieve and return the article to the handler. Often, the first article they are taught to pick up is their own treat box – needless to say, this task is quickly learned! The teaching process is based on the reward method. Vocal and physical praise, food and play are used to motivate the dog and encourage a good response.

Most of the breeds used are very food-oriented; the Labrador and the Golden Retriever will do most things asked of them for a tasty reward! Initially, food is given to reward a response every time a task is carried out. Intermittent reward follows once the response is established, to keep the dog really interested and keen. Play incentive is used, but not all dogs are motivated by play and some handlers find the timing and effort required difficult to maintain.

More recently, the training staff have been experimenting with 'clicker' and 'target' training. This American training method is beginning to prove very successful when training future Dogs for the Disabled (page 72).

Dogs are taught the following obedience and control commands: "Sit", "Down", "Stay", "Wait", "Heel", "No", "Leave", "On your bed", "Steady", "Back", and the command for the dog to relieve himself "Busy". They also learn basic task commands which are: to pull, jump up, press or push, pick up and bark on command.

BASIC COMMANDS

Pull
Is a modification on the game tug-of-war. It is used for opening or closing doors, emptying washing machines and activating emergency alarm cords.

Jump up
This is taught on command rather than as a bad habit. It would be used to retrieve articles from a high surface, to pass a purse or wallet over a counter or to return a dropped article on to the owner's lap or into his hand.

Press or push
To operate light switches or activate push buttons, e.g. for lifts or electric doors on trains and telephone alarm buttons.

Pick up
To retrieve items, such as letters, post, the newspaper or any named articles. A named article is something that is requested regularly, such as a cordless telephone, slippers, the television remote control or a handbag. The dog will learn the item's name and will be able to fetch it on request. The dog is also taught to pick up articles accidentally dropped by the owner, such as keys, crutches or gloves.

Speak or bark on command
The dog is taught to bark on command to attract attention and/or to raise the alarm if the owner is in difficulty.

Additional commands or specialist training appropriate to the client's needs would be undertaken once the dog has been matched to his new owner.

A Dog for the Disabled learning to walk at the correct pace next to a wheelchair.

WHEELCHAIR TRAINING

A Dog for the Disabled must be taught to walk steadily beside a wheelchair in any environment, quiet or busy. Getting too close to the chair could result in the dog having his feet run over. The dog is encouraged to walk beside the chair at a steady pace. The speed of travel is then increased as the dog gains more confidence next to the chair.

The degree to which the new owner can use his hands and arms will dictate whether the dog walks on the right or the left of the wheelchair. Some dogs are attached by the lead to the owner's arm, rather than the hand, especially in the case of a person having little or no grip, or if they need a hands-free situation to steer or wheel their chair.

Kerbs, lifts and ramps, giving access to shops and buildings, have to be negotiated carefully; the dog must never be fearful of the wheelchair. The dog is taught to stop at kerbs and to negotiate obstacles. He is taught to sit or lie down quietly while the owner is shopping, choosing, queuing or talking. But the dog has to be ready to pass a purse over or pick up something dropped. Repetition is the only way to get the dog behaving confidently in these situations, gradually building on the tasks required to achieve the end result.

For disabled people that use crutches, it is just as important that the dog learns to walk steadily beside the owner without pulling. It could not be described as precision heel-work, but it is vital that the dog remains beside the person on a slack lead. The command "Heel" can be used if the dog is getting too far ahead.

TRAINING IN PUBLIC AREAS

When out training in public areas, the dog will wear a blue jacket. This helps to identify him to members of the public and shop-keepers alike. The dog will be allowed access to places other dogs are not normally allowed to enter, such as the library, food stores, public buildings and shopping precincts.

Identifying working dogs in this way also helps to educate the public, in an effort to encourage people not to distract or feed the dogs while working. This is crucial to the safety of the dog and owner – a dog that is not concentrating on the job in hand may become more of a hazard than a help.

The dog has to be confident working in any environment. His new owner may need to travel by bus or train to work, or to visit family and friends, and these are all situations that the dog has to learn to take in his stride.

It is important that the dog is trained in busy, public areas too.

The dog will understandably receive a lot of attention and must learn to accept the well-deserved praise in a calm, friendly manner. He must behave himself at all times. Jumping up, barking, getting on furniture, or helping himself to food is not acceptable. The dog is taken on trips to cafes, pubs and restaurants to teach him to lie quietly under the table out of sight without scavenging. It is hoped that seeing a dog behaving well in this type of environment will encourage other shop owners and managers to allow assistance dogs into places where they would normally be excluded.

TEACHING THE COMMANDS

PULL

To teach the dog to pull, first you have to teach the rules of tug-of-war. Most dogs love this game and are quick to learn. Tug-of-war is a very physical, interactive game that will display just how much control you have over your dog. With a motivating toy, the dog is encouraged to pull and is praised for doing so. When the dog is really attached to the toy and looks as if he will never let go, offer a tasty treat directly in front of his nose and, as he lets go, command "Give". The toy is then re-offered to the dog and, as the dog takes hold and starts to tug, the command "Pull/hold" is given. Eventually, various articles of different texture will be presented to the dog to pull on, especially during the specialist training phase.

This command will eventually be associated with:
• Pulling a rope attached to a door handle.
• Pulling long cords which operate the light switch or emergency alarm.
• Pulling washing out of a machine.
• Pulling clothes off.

Once the dog has pulled the relevant article, he is immediately rewarded with vocal and physical praise as well as a treat.

It is amazing how quickly the dog will learn to put his head in the washing machine, especially if he has found a few treats in there to start with. Learning to pull the clothes out is the next step. This is done through retrieve – asking the dog to bring the clothes to the owner.

To get the dog to open doors, he has to

Pulling a wheelchair or opening a door by pulling a rope is an extension of the tug game.

associate going through the door with a good experience. Getting him to nudge open or "Push" a partially open door to retrieve a favourite toy or his treat box is an ideal stimulus.

Once the dog is doing this enthusiastically, the task is made more difficult, and the dog has to learn to pull an attached rope. The door will only be partially closed, so minimal effort is required, with an immediate reward on the other side.

A fun game of tug-of-war is the first step to teaching the pull command.

Pulling at the rope is similar to the tug-of-war game and is quickly achieved. Eventually, the dog is able to open a closed door by pulling on the rope to operate the handle and to continue pulling the door open wide. If the door opens away from you once the handle has been operated, the dog then has to push the door open wide. To close the door, the push/pull command is used.

THE RETRIEVE

The dog's natural desire to retrieve and pull are developed in training. The retrieve is a combination of exercises and can be broken down into individual components. It is essential that the dog enjoys retrieving and should not become disinterested if the exercise is repeated. To get a dog totally focused on carrying out the retrieve, a favourite toy or article may be used initially to develop a keen response.

The retrieve task is broken down into stages of learning, and the learned aspects are then linked together to complete the task. The retrieve is a combination of three commands: "Hold/fetch" the named article, "Come" and "Give".

The dog is encouraged to play with the article he is about to retrieve and must be highly motivated by the mere sight of the object. He is praised for holding or picking up the article. Once the dog is highly motivated at the sight of the article, it is then offered to the dog for him to

"Hold". The dog is praised and then asked to "Give" (tug-of-war helps to develop the "Hold" and "Give" commands).

The article is then thrown a short distance. The dog is praised for touching, holding or picking up the article. The dog quickly learns that these actions are approved of and that it is good fun to pick up the object. He will gradually hold on to the article for longer periods and should be praised the whole time he has the article in his mouth. Should the dog spit the article out, the handler should stop praising and remotivate him to pick up the article again. If tug-of-war has been taught successfully, the dog should return to you because he associates you with having a game. As the dog approaches the trainer, the "Come" command is given. He is praised profusely for returning to the handler while still holding on to the toy.

The handler should then take hold of the article without pulling. The dog is then told to "Give". In the initial stages of learning, the article should be thrown as soon as the dog has given it to you. The reward for giving, at this stage, is the article being thrown again. In the advanced stage, the reward would be a treat.

Once the dog is retrieving enthusiastically, the article is changed, and eventually the dog is taught to pick up a variety of items: different-sized pens, gloves, bags, keys, slippers, shoes, walking sticks, crutches and keys – the list goes on and on. Once the dog is retrieving a variety of different articles, the game will become more natural. Dropping items will be introduced, and learning to retrieve named items will also be developed.

PRESS OR PUSH
Usually the dog is taught to press a light switch or button with his foot. Some equipment, such as a telephone alarm button, benefits from a more delicate touch. If more precise targeting is required, then the dog is taught to use his nose. Clicker and target training (see page 72) are used to teach targeting.

SPEAK ON COMMAND
In situations where the disabled person may fall in the street or in their home, the need to alert someone is paramount. Every dog is different when it comes to encouraging them to bark. Some will copy a dog that has already been taught to "Speak". Some will need to be excited in some way to encourage them to make a sound; seeing

ABOVE: The trainee is praised each time he holds an item.

RIGHT: Eventually the dog will be able to fetch and hold a whole range of articles.

Once the dog has mastered the push command at the training centre, he can be taken out to practise in public areas.

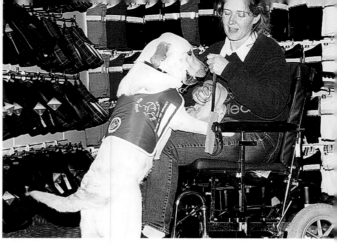

Sometimes it is necessary for the dog to jump up. This dog is returning a dropped bag to his trainer.

their lead, or anticipating a walk or a game is a successful method. However small the first amount of noise the dog makes, he will be commanded to "Speak" and then praised and rewarded. It does not take long for most dogs to get the idea.

JUMP UP

Most dogs are keen to jump up, but this common habit could be dangerous to a disabled person, especially someone who uses crutches. During training, any unrequested jumping up would be discouraged. But jumping up does have its uses. If done on command, it can enable the dog to reach something for his owner or pass over a purse at a counter. The command is first taught by applying the command "Up" as the dog is being encouraged to jump up to retrieve a favourite article or toy. It is then extended to retrieving a named article and then returning it to the instructor who is sitting in a wheelchair. The dog will be given permission to jump up, either with his front feet on the lap or front feet on the arm of the wheelchair. This enables the person to take the retrieved item without stretching towards the dog. This is an excellent service for people with limited mobility in their hands or arms.

CLICKER AND TARGET TRAINING

Clicker training is a method of marking a response and then rewarding it with a favourite treat. The clicker is a small, plastic box containing a steel spring. When pressed, it makes a sharp clicking noise, hence the name.

Dogs for the Disabled is currently using clicker and target training methods to teach specific tasks with some dogs. This is where the dog is taught to touch a 'target stick', a 12-inch wand, with his foot or nose. The clicker is pressed, and the dog is rewarded. Once the dog is keen to touch the target stick, the dog will be taught to follow it, so he can be lured into a desired position or place. He can also be encouraged to touch other articles or carry out an action, such as pressing a button, pushing a door, or activating an emergency alarm. It can also be used to teach the dog the correct walking position beside the wheelchair and to teach him to retrieve.

The clicker marks the moment the dog makes the response you require. In the dog's mind, he quickly learns that the action performed gets a reward. When training, it is crucial to have the right mood, tone of voice and body language. The clicker has no moods, no voice that lacks genuine praise, or disappointed body language. It is a very positive, precise form of indicating correct behaviour, reinforced with a treat. Some sensitive dogs that seem slow to learn or reluctant to respond usually thrive with this approach to training. The dog seems to gain a more positive attitude to training overnight.

Introduction to clicker training will involve one of three different approaches:

• **Developing a behaviour**
The dog can be lured into the desired position before clicking and treating. The desired behaviour can be shaped or created step-by-step, clicking and treating each small step in the right

direction to the final goal. An alternative method can be to watch for a desired behaviour and then click and treat, e.g. lure the dog into his bed, then click and treat.

- **Shaping a behaviour**

To encourage a dog to go to his bed you would click the dog for taking a step towards it, and continue to click and treat as the dog progressively gets closer to the bed.

- **Watching**

The handler waits for the dog to go to his bed and then clicks and treats. Once the dog is repeating the desired behaviour reliably, and is prepared to repeat the response without being rewarded every time, it is time to add the command to the behaviour.

SPECIALIST TRAINING

Once the dog has been matched to his new owner, the instructor can concentrate on additional tasks that will be required of the dog. Usually it is a task that is just an extension of the basic training exercises. The pulling task may be used to help undress the recipient, pulling socks and trousers off. In the case study featured earlier in the book. Tara has learned to pull a leather strap that is fitted around the lower part of her owner's leg. By pulling this strap, Tara is able to move her owner's legs across the bed. Other dogs may be taught to carry a shopping basket, bring in the milk-crate from the front door, or pass a purse over the counter to a shop assistant.

One working dog has been taught to take his owner's shopping basket and list into a shop. This is done independently of his owner as the shop has a large step outside which is impossible to negotiate with a wheelchair. The dog then carries the basket containing the shopping back to his owner, who is waiting outside.

Another dog has been taught to retrieve all the relevant pieces of a hoist, which has to be moved from the bedroom to the bathroom. Once the sling hoist is assembled, the dog's owner can bath or use the lavatory without the help of a carer. The dog enables the owner to maintain her independence and self-esteem.

Wearing a special harness, a Dog for the Disabled can be taught to help an owner with balance difficulties to move about more easily. The dog does not actually take the weight of the person, but the close proximity of the dog's

Carrying the shopping is one of the specialist tasks that Dogs for the Disabled can be taught.

With the help of a special harness, some dogs can be taught to help their owners overcome their balance and stability problems.

body to the owner acts like a prop, which is sufficient support to give them the balance and stability to propel themselves forward or to move from one position to another. It takes a special type of dog to do this work: they are usually large, relaxed and confident dogs, that are bodily resilient and enjoy physical contact.

The needs of each disabled person are different, so the dogs have to be taught a variety of specialist tasks. After starting life at home with a new owner, the ability and versatility of the dog develops. In time, as confidence grows and a rapport builds between dog and owner, many owners have to think hard when asked exactly what it is that the dog does for them. Their work together has become so automatic, the partnership has developed almost unconsciously. A dog is consistent – he does not get bored with repetitive tasks, is always willing, and gives unquestioning loyalty to his owner.

Having the dog presents the new owner with all the responsibilities of dog ownership. Feeding, grooming and general care of the dog are all new techniques that have to be learned. Daily exercise is essential for the dog, of course. This exercise is also beneficial for the new owner – it is a reason to go out. Many recipients relate how much more exercise and fresh air they get after obtaining a dog and through the dog making more contact with other people.

People are often reluctant to approach a disabled person, for fear of saying the wrong thing and causing embarrassment to themselves or to the disabled person. In the same way that a Guide Dog facilitates communication, a Dog for the Disabled also bridges the gap. People will stop and talk because of the dog. For a disabled person living alone, the opportunity to communicate with people can be limited.

Outings with the dog often initiate conversation and contact and this interaction is something from which everyone benefits. Talking and laughing with other people is a wonderful tonic. There are few genuine loners in this world!

RETIREMENT OF A DOG FOR THE DISABLED

There is no set age for retirement. The dog and owner will be visited and assessed regularly throughout the dog's working life, and once he reaches the age of eight years, his health and willingness to work will be closely monitored. Existing clients are given priority on the waiting list to ensure that a replacement dog is found as quickly as possible. If an overlap cannot be achieved, then time without a dog is kept to a minimum. The charity has a responsibility to its existing owners to continue to provide the service they have come to rely on. A dog-less existence would affect the owner's quality of life dramatically.

If the owner's home circumstances permit, the client may be allowed to keep the retired dog as a pet. However, if this is not possible, the organisation will find the dog a suitable home. Sometimes a retired dog will go back to his original puppy-walker. Dogs for the Disabled also has a waiting list of people who have applied to care for a rejected or retired dog. All these people are carefully assessed before being accepted.

The success of a charity can be measured by how effective it is in meeting the needs of those it was set up to assist. Judged by this criterion, Dogs for the Disabled is well on the way to satisfying the needs of those who have approached it for help.

CASE HISTORY

SUE LEE AND NINJA

Name: Sue Lee.
Dog for the Disabled: Ninja, a Rottweiler.
Family: Recently married.
Occupation/interests: Fund-raising for Dogs for the Disabled.

Ninja's story shows that, with careful training, dogs can be rehabilitated to become the ultimate home-help.

Sue was trained by well-known dog behaviourist John Rogerson. She attended many of his courses and went on to become a behaviourist herself. It was in the course of her work that Sue became disabled.

While she was out walking a large Newfoundland that was difficult to control, the dog suddenly took a lunge at a passing car. Sue fell heavily and suffered severe spinal injuries and spent a long time in a wheelchair. She is now able to walk with crutches. Sue's left leg is wasted and she is unable to bend from the waist, but she is able to live a more independent lifestyle with the assistance of Ninja, the Rottweiler.

' I rescued Ninja when he was nine months old. I already had an old Rottweiler bitch and felt it was time to look for a youngster. Through a vet, I heard about a dog who had been found in a forest, tied to a tree and left. He had been found a foster home in a house full of Rottweilers; although breed enthusiasts, they felt they couldn't cope with another male.

"Ninja already had the reputation of being savage and uncontrollable, and the last thing I wanted was an aggressive dog, but I took one look at the large, boisterous male strutting around the garden and knew he was the dog for me.

"My experience as a dog trainer helped me to assess Ninja. It didn't take long for me to realise that this dog had potential. Here was a large dog who had obviously taken advantage of his previous owners. But his intelligence and enthusiasm to work shone through, and I knew it was a case of channelling this attitude and willingness into something useful.

"Ninja and I attended many John Rogerson courses and his character and ability rapidly developed. Everyone that met Ninja would comment on his wonderful nature. Wherever I went with him, he took it all in his stride. People, cats, horses, new places and other dogs, he was friendly and confident with them all.

"Ninja was four years old when I had my accident, and our daily routine was turned

Ninja was such a help after Sue had her accident, that she encouraged him to learn more tasks.

upside down. How was I going to manage? My friends had been so helpful when I was in hospital. One had kept an eye on the house for me, another had looked after Ninja. At the time, I lived in a quiet village, but after the accident Ninja and I needed the help and support of friends and family, so I moved to Bournemouth where help was at hand.

"Once out of the wheelchair and more mobile with the use of a walking frame, I realised just how supportive Ninja was. He was always at my side, prepared to guide me gently. But I felt guilty – I didn't want to use him as a support dog. I am a large lady and using Ninja in this way would not have been fair.

"I worked hard to improve my mobility and once out of the wheelchair, I was able to get about using crutches. Almost unconsciously, I found myself encouraging Ninja to pick up my crutches if I accidentally dropped one. He loved it, so I started to teach him a few other tasks, such as emptying the washing machine and picking up the post and newspaper, all things I couldn't do because I can't bend.

"It is not until you are unable to do something that you realise just how valuable mobility is. Getting things stored on a low shelf, picking up the television remote control when it falls on the floor, tidying up after you have undressed – all are very difficult tasks

when your movement is restricted.

"Ninja proved his loyalty to me after an accident that occurred while walking in the New Forest. I was now able to drive an automatic car and enjoyed taking Ninja to the forest to let off steam. I would walk as far as I could, usually off the beaten track. Although these routes are more difficult to negotiate, they are much more interesting for the dog.

"It was on one of these treks that I fell and broke my leg below the knee. I was stranded and in dreadful pain, and Ninja instinctively came to my side. I knew the only way to get out was to hold on to Ninja's collar and slowly hop on my good leg back to the car-park to get help. It took ages. Ninja never rushed or stopped, he just steadily kept going, until we reached the car-park and, thankfully, there were people in sight.

"Because Ninja wasn't an official Dog for the Disabled, there were certain places where I couldn't take him. Ninja was prohibited from access to shops and public buildings, and visiting the library and any public function. It was very frustrating having to leave him at home and then rely on people helping me in these situations, so I decided to try to get Ninja officially recognised.

"It took me six months to persuade George Cram, instructor for the Dogs for the Disabled organisation, to come and assess

Ninja in attendance on Sue and Dave's big day.

Ninja. He was very reluctant to register Ninja the Rottweiler because of public anti-breed feeling. Would the dog be a good representative for the organisation? Once registered, Dogs for the Disabled would be responsible for any publicity, good or bad, that Ninja may create. A privately trained dog may prove to be more of a liability than a help.

"Unbeknown to me, I already had a reputation with the organisation. They had heard a lot about the Rottweiler that had been trained by his owner. They were also impressed with my dog-training qualifications. With this knowledge and, bearing in mind the many favourable comments they had received, Dogs for the Deaf decided to assess us, but no promises were made.

"The assessor, Caroline Bull, instantly fell in love with the cuddly giant, but knew she had to put him through his paces and report back before a decision could be made. Caroline observed me and Ninja doing our household tasks and she was impressed with the wide range of tasks the dog carried out with enthusiasm – emptying the washing machine, collecting the post and the paper, picking up a range of articles from shoes to a bunch of keys...

"Lots of varied items were deliberately dropped for the test, but I held my breath when the phone rang. I had only recently taught Ninja this task. It was a new telephone with a cradle attachment for Ninja to get hold of. He had picked it up plenty of times to enable me to make a call, but he was still a little hesitant to pick it up when it was ringing! I need not have worried: he made it look as if he had been doing it all his life. He picked it up and swaggered across the room to me and placed it in my lap, I'm sure he was showing off, but nevertheless he got a huge hug for doing it!

"I knew the big test would come when we took him into town. I was aware that Caroline was concerned about how Ninja would behave in public. At home was one thing; out on the streets was something completely different. Caroline asked, 'How does he behave in crowds?' 'Is he good with children?' 'Is he frightened by traffic?' I knew he was perfectly behaved in all these situations, but would she agree?

"Ninja walked beside me at his usual steady pace. I explained to Caroline that if he gets too far ahead, I tell him "Back!" and he then drops back into position beside me, which I demonstrated. I hoped this was a good start to the test route. We had to walk through a department store, to stop and browse. Ninja lay on the floor quietly. We then had to have a cup of coffee in a cafe to check Ninja's behaviour. He lay under the table and didn't attempt to scrounge from me or anyone else in the cafe; again he lay quietly. Our last stop was buying a magazine in the newsagent. I was so nervous because I didn't want my dog to fail. In fact, Ninja had to pick up my purse twice because I kept dropping it.

"During the test, Ninja drew a lot of attention. So many people stopped to talk to us, and most of them asked if they could stroke him. People were attracted to him like magnet. Ninja was obviously in his element, he loved all the attention and praise that came his way. He just sat patiently, absorbing all the adoration!

"The most crucial part of the test happened

unexpectedly. We had just come out of a shop and the three of us were walking down the High Street, when a dog appeared from nowhere and lunged, barking and growling at Ninja. I was a little startled but Ninja didn't even break stride, let alone look at the dog or bark back. It was the sort of unexpected incident that an assistance dog has to learn to ignore and Ninja did. I am sure it was at this point that Caroline was convinced he should qualify as a Dog for the Disabled. We had to wait for a few weeks and have one more test to ensure Ninja wasn't just having a good day. Then at the age of six, he was presented with his official yellow jacket. He is a different dog when he's got his jacket on. He knows the difference between being on and off duty.

"I recently got married to Dave, who is also disabled. We had to gain permission to take Ninja to the registry office. The day would not have been the same without him. When we went to the office to apply for permission, they expected to see a Labrador or Golden Retriever, and did a double-take when we walked in with a Rottweiler. But Ninja, as usual, stole the show, becoming the centre of attention. With permission granted and an extra carnation booked for Ninja, we are looking forward to the big day.

"Ninja is one of three independently trained Dogs for the Disabled. He has become an ambassador for the organisation and the breed. He nearly always converts the doubters of this world – that even a Rottweiler, a dog associated with guarding and police work, can be a successful Dog for the Disabled.

"Like most other dogs, Ninja loves a cuddle and plenty of affection. He is evidence that with considerate handling, time and patience, even the most misunderstood dog can achieve anything in the right hands.

"Ninja is now eight years old. Like most Rottweilers, especially the big ones, his life-expectancy is not much more than ten. My condition has deteriorated, and I no longer feel that I am able to train a dog in the future. So when the time comes, I will rely on Dogs for the Disabled to find me a suitable replacement. I am not looking forward to that day – Ninja will be a hard act to follow. *,*

4 THERAPY DOGS

Early in 1974, B. M. Levinson, a New York professor of psychology, presented a paper at a symposium held in London. As part of his speech he attempted to forecast what life would be like in the year 2000. He predicted that as human relationships became increasingly stressed, people would turn more to companion animals for stability. He foresaw an animal lending service, for mental health and welfare, available on prescription for the sick and disabled. Little did he know how his ideas would develop.

Today, hundreds of owners take their dogs on visits to hospitals, hospices, residential homes and to schools, where the residents or pupils can share some time with a dog, and benefit from the companionship and affection a dog can offer. A quarter of a century on, and Mr Levinson's predictions for the future seem very much to have materialised.

HISTORY OF THE THERAPY DOG

In the USA, pioneering work was started in 1980 by the American Humane Association on a list of organisations that were interested in pet-facilitated therapy. This resulted in the Pet Partner programme, founded by the Delta Society, which now has representatives in 45 states across the USA, and a total of more than 2,000 Pet Partner teams.

Considerable resistance was met when a similar scheme was introduced in the UK. Concerns had to be overcome about the health implications of introducing dogs to hospital wards, or allowing dogs to come into such close contact with children. Lesley Scott-Ordish, who worked and campaigned tirelessly on behalf of dogs, set up the charity, Pets As Therapy, in 1983. She had to fight for it to be recognised that, far from being a

danger, dogs could actually improve health and well-being.

Fear that animals posed a health risk was given extensive press coverage. Reports claimed that dogs were infested with toxocara canis. Others stated that 2.5 per cent of the population are made ill from worm-infested dogs, and that it could cause illness or even blindness if a person became infected. These were all irrational, yet frightening, stories that the newspapers published!

Lesley set about proving that the statistics quoted were inaccurate and misleading, and that research could show humans were at little or no risk when coming into contact with dogs. More than a hundred multi-dog owners were blood-tested and asked to fill in a questionnaire. The samples were analysed and they proved that, even if people that had been in contact with this

Lesley Scott-Ordish visiting a patient at Maidstone Hospital, Kent, with PAT Dog Ella.

Contact with animals not only lifts the spirit and produces happier residents, it also has significant health benefits.

parasite, they had not been made ill or even been aware of any illness.

In an effort to inform the public, Lesley also worked at producing a booklet, which is still available today, explaining just what happens if a tiny toxocaral egg accidentally gets inside a person.

"People are not natural hosts of this parasite and therefore the worm can never develop and multiply inside the human body," Lesley wrote. As well as explaining the life-cycle of the worm, the booklet, also includes important advice on an effective worming programme for dogs and puppies, which is the best way to reduce any risk associated with this parasite.

The research and subsequent opportunity to broadcast the findings on radio and television was a turning point in public awareness and in the attitude of the medical profession towards dogs. The uphill struggle to persuade the medical establishment to accept dogs within hospital environments began to have an effect. Medical consultants eventually agreed that the risks of infection to patients was far greater from the humans accompanying the dog than the dog itself. Medical evaluation studies have been, and are still being, undertaken to measure the more significant benefits that have already been recorded.

To support the growing evidence that dogs seemed to make their owners feel better, a questionnaire was published in a UK canine newspaper. More than 1,500 questionnaires were analysed. The overwhelming result showed that dogs helped their owners' everyday health and

well-being. The dogs won hands down.

Since then, Pets As Therapy has continued to carry out valuable studies. Research has established that stroking a pet lowers the heart rate and is beneficial for people suffering from heart disease. Conclusions of a combined study highlighted that a massive 99 per cent of dog owners who were asked, believed that owning a dog had improved their quality of life:

- The loyalty and affection shown by the dogs made them feel good.
- Touching, stroking and grooming the dog gave mutual pleasure to owner and dog.
- A huge majority of dog owners (94 per cent) said that owning a dog improved their

It is now commonly recognised that contact with pets is beneficial to a person's health and well-being.

quality of life. It encouraged them to take part in activities, such as training classes, showing, or obedience competitions, and many other dog-related events in which they would not have otherwise participated.

Shortly after the therapy dog visiting scheme began, the matron of a residential home in Kent noticed that the visits of a therapy dog called Rosie had a calming effect on a hyperactive patient. She asked if the dog could visit in the evenings to help the lady settle more calmly at night. The effect was amazing. Touching and stroking not only calmed the lady, but she would relax entirely and enjoy a full night's sleep.

Some of the other residents relied on sleeping tablets. Could it be that the people who enjoyed stroking the dog could be weaned off their drugs? One such patient, John, was visited every night for ten weeks by therapy dog Questor. The dog was substituted as the drugs were gradually withdrawn. The experiment was entirely successful. For the last four years of John's life, he was able to sleep longer and naturally without drugs, and said he felt livelier in the daytime.

As more success stories were recorded and media reporting became much more sympathetic, the membership of Pets As Therapy grew. Now the professionals within the health service are regularly requesting therapy dog visits for people who are lonely or withdrawn or for those that are hospitalised and miss their pets. Residential homes for the elderly, children, and adults, have all recognised that residents respond to the presence of a dog – whether it is just to talk to and stroke the dog or to help with the rehabilitation of patients through mental stimulation or physiotherapy. Dogs, and now cats, too, are providing therapy, comfort and affection to many.

CASE HISTORY

CAROLINE DAWSON AND TANNER

Name: Caroline Dawson.
PAT Dog: Tanner, a Border Collie.

Realising how Tanner had helped to improve her own morale, Caroline thought that Tanner could help others too.

Caroline was born with a congenital heart condition and developed scoliosis by the age of four. As a child, Caroline found it difficult to take part in some of the more physical aspects of being young and active. But after a seven-hour operation on her spine, and further cardiac complications, her general physical condition and ability to partake in sports became limited. She spent most of her childhood and teenage years going in and out of hospital. On being discharged yet again from hospital, her specialist raised an eyebrow when Caroline announced she was going to get herself a Border Collie. Despite his misgivings, she was determined to go ahead.

'I had previously owned a Border Collie, so had a good idea of the dog's need for exercise and mental stimulation. I am aware of the Border Collie's requirements regarding training, motivation and human companionship. I knew I could exercise a dog twice a day with a ball or Frisbee in an open field, even on my bad days when I need to conserve energy.

"Tanner was eight months old when I got him. He had been bred as a prospective show dog, but although he was handsome, with a reliable friendly temperament, his breeder felt he was not quite suitable for the show ring. Tanner quickly settled in and enjoyed his new lifestyle as my constant companion.

"I was amazed by his delightful temperament. He loves children and he takes everything in his stride, everything we do and everywhere we go – he enjoys it all. He's so laid back, he often borders on being lazy!

Caroline knew it would be a challenge to keep up with a Border Collie, but she also knew the rewards made it worthwhile.

"Tanner is as sensitive to my needs and limitations as I am to his. When I had an accident in the park, Tanner stood beside me on guard until my family arrived. He also became very distressed when I cried out in pain as the paramedics moved me into the ambulance.

"Thanks to Tanner, I am now walking a minimum of two miles a day and we both participate in Agility, though Tanner will never win any prizes while I'm handling him, as he slows up and waits for me! Additionally, my cardiac consultant who once expressed so much concern about me owning a dog, now realises the benefits and always asks after Tanner when I visit him for my regular check-ups.

"I started to think that Tanner may be able to help others, too – especially after a certain incident that happened. Tanner was having a rough and tumble in the park with my nieces and nephew, when an eight-year-old girl asked if she could join in. The child had never had anything to do with a dog before. She suffered from brittle bone disease and had been in hospital many times for fractures to various bones in her body.

"I put Tanner on the lead as he had become quite excited while playing with the other children. I did not want him to be boisterous with the girl and knock her over. Her parents were torn between worrying about the possible outcome and the strong desire not to wrap their daughter in cotton wool. Standing close to the girl so I could step in if it started to go wrong, I handed the child Tanner's lead. We were all amazed to see Tanner walk quietly and calmly at her side, ignoring the other children and the rough game they were having a few moments before. He seemed to sense the girl's needs and quickly adjusted to the circumstances he found himself in. I will never forget the smile on the girl's face – my dog had given her so much pleasure.

"Tanner passed his assessment to become a therapy dog with flying colours. I decided to concentrate on working with children, as Tanner was so good with them. Tanner always takes his Frisbee on his visits, in case there is a

Tanner's love of retrieving toys provides a fun game in which patients can exercise their muscles in an enjoyable way.

child able and interested enough to play with him. After a few weeks of visiting the children in hospital, it became apparent that Tanner's love of games could be used to encourage patients with limited movement to work at exercising their limbs to increase their co-ordination and mobility. Patients are able to exercise their arms when throwing the Frisbee for Tanner, and he quickly returns the toy to their lap for the game to be repeated."

A physiotherapist explains: "The exercise regimes are often painful, boring and at times seem pointless to the patient. Anything that encourages and motivates a patient to try harder and keep at it, is welcomed by the therapists and nurses. Some patients have to be propped in a standing frame to gain strength in their backs. Tanner soon worked out that if he stood on his hind legs, he could place the Frisbee on the table at the front of the frame, however high it was. The patients reward the dog by throwing the toy for him, Tanner never gets bored with this repetitive game."

"Tanner's love of playing tug-of-war with his Frisbee or his lead is a useful exercise for patients who have to learn to grip again after suffering from a stroke or surgery to their hands," says Caroline. "One young girl, who

had to have skin grafts to her hands, was playing tug enthusiastically with Tanner. The nurses were delighted – they had been trying for days to get the child to squeeze her hand in and out!

"Patients, especially children, are often reluctant to co-operate with the physiotherapists because of the pain associated with the exercises. Playing games with Tanner is always a good distraction. A young boy had major surgery after serious injury to his legs and was in a lot of pain. He refused to move for his physio, but he decided he wanted to join in the games. He got out of his bed with the use of crutches took a few steps to pick up the Frisbee and throw it. The boy later said, 'I thought about playing with Tanner and the pain would disappear!'

"All sorts of difficult exercises for the patient can be made into a game with Tanner. An 11-year-old girl, who really loved Tanner's visits was having trouble finding the motivation to practise moving from her wheelchair to her bed. This manoeuvre was an important part of her rehabilitation programme. I had the idea of making it a race. Tanner would wait at the end of the ward and when all was clear and permission was granted, he would race her to get on to the bed. Initially, the patient was given a good head-start, but practice was necessary between visits because she knew the distance of the head-start would be shortened on Tanner's next visit. The effect was amazing – she was soon scrambling from the chair into her bed in no time.

"His work with a particular teenage girl will be remembered by all who were involved. The girl had suffered serious head injuries during a horrific road accident. She was severely disabled, her speech was limited, she was confined to a wheelchair and needed a great deal of physiotherapy to regain some movement of her hands. The young girl found it difficult to accept her injuries and would be stubborn and refuse to co-operate with the nursing staff trying to rehabilitate her.

"The only thing she did look forward to was Tanner's visits and she would watch from a distance as Tanner played his games with other

Pushing treats across the table towards Tanner helped one girl to exercise her hand and arm muscles.

patients. Even if our friend was not joining in, it did not take long for Tanner to work his magic and bring her out of her depression. Interacting with Tanner encouraged her to exercise her paralysed hands. By pushing her chair to a table, she was then able to play her own special game with him. It was also a first for Tanner, as he was allowed to sit on a chair at the table next to the girl.

"We would put treats in her hand, which encouraged her to grip, and then she had to laboriously push the treat across the table to Tanner. This proved to be an excellent way to get her to give much-needed exercise to her hands and arms and was thoroughly enjoyed by the patient and Tanner.

"Tanner is always a boost to the patients' morale. Even for those that feel life can't get much worse, he works his special kind of magic. **"**

HOW TO BECOME A THERAPY DOG

There are numerous organisations and individuals that work in the growing field of therapy dogs. For a dog to become a PAT Dog, the dog and owner have to be registered members of PRO Dogs. This ensures that if the dog qualifies, he will then be covered by the PRO Dogs' insurance policy. Pedigree, mongrel or crossbreed, any shape, size or parentage will suit! As long as the dog is friendly with people, has a relaxed attitude to life, and the owner has some time to spare on a regular basis, then they may both be suitable.

The dog must be at least six months old or have been in the care of his owner for that length of time. It is important that the owner should know the dog inside out and that the two of them have developed a trusting relationship. The owner should be able to recognise if the dog is unhappy in any situation they have placed themselves in. Even the best behaved dogs have off days!

Specialised training, such as obedience work, is a bonus but is not essential. As long as the dog is friendly, is under control, is well behaved on the lead and is past the unruly, jumping-up stage, he may be suitable. Rough, boisterous behaviour displayed by some dogs could be dangerous to an elderly or frail person; this type of dog would be unsuitable. If the dog is excitable due to youth, or a lack of education, the owner would be encouraged to re-apply at a later stage. Once the dog has matured and calmed down, and control has been developed, the application would more likely be successful.

THE INITIAL APPLICATION

The application form has to be completed by the owner, and a recognised official has to carry out the required temperament and behaviour test on the dog. The information provided on the form tells the organisation all about the dog and owner: breed, age, training experience, etc. Other questions include whether the dog behaves well in the company of adults and children, whether the owner is certain he can control the dog in a variety of situations, and whether the dog will respond accordingly. The form also includes a section for the owner's personal assessment of the dog's temperament.

In addition, the dog must have a current vaccination certificate. No unvaccinated dog can be accepted as a therapy dog. The organisation's insurance policy will not allow them to accept dogs that have been vaccinated homoeopathically. There is not enough clinical evidence that this approach to protecting a dog against disease is effective.

The organisation has a few Guide Dog owners and their dogs registered as therapy dogs. The owner of any dog belonging to Guide Dogs for the Blind (whether a Guide Dog, breeding stock or a dog being puppy-walked) must have the

A therapy dog should be confident and relaxed when handled.

agreement of the Guide Dogs' charity before applying for it to become a therapy dog.

TEMPERAMENT TEST

The final part of the application is to have the dog's temperament tested by a recognised official. This can be a veterinary surgeon, a Pets As Therapy co-ordinator, a dog training instructor, a practising animal nurse, a qualified dog groomer or a member of the Guide Dogs' training staff. The questions involved in testing a potential therapy dog include:

1) Assess the dog's manner of approach. Is the dog happy to come to you when called?
2) Is the tail and head carriage: normal/high/low?
3) Is the dog over-boisterous in greeting or normally friendly?
4) Does the dog show any signs of nervousness or aggression?
5) Is the dog calm and gentle when stroked?
6) How does the dog react to a loud noise simulating a dropped walking stick or crutch?
7) If the dog backs away, does he re-approach readily if asked?
8) How does the dog react to an examination of his ears, tail and body? Is he relaxed or worried?
9) Will the dog sit and wait?
10) How does the dog take treats: gently/snatches/refuses?
11) Does the dog generally appear relaxed and happy?

As with all assistance dogs, a reliable, friendly, confident temperament is the dog's most important asset. A therapy dog must not show any sign of aggression or apprehension. He must not snatch if treats are offered, he must be relaxed and confident when handled, and should not over-react to sudden noises or unexpected approaches from people. He should also be under control at all times throughout a visit.

The Golden Retriever is the most popular breed actively working at present as a therapy dog. Second is the Labrador Retriever, and the Border Collie is in third place. There are also numerous variations of crossbreeds that qualify.

Therapy dog Jasper has the calm character needed to pass the temperament test.

CASE HISTORY

SYLVIA HUMPHRIES AND CLYDE
JACKIE COOK AND SIMBA

Names: Sylvia Humphries and Jackie Cook.
PAT Dogs: Clyde and Simba, both Golden Retrievers.

Tanner (Page 81) is not the only dog visiting a special unit. Simba and Clyde, two large Golden Retriever males, are regular visitors to the Neuro Head Injury ward at the Royal National Hospital for Rheumatic Diseases in Bath.

This department cares for patients suffering from head injuries or neurological illnesses. Adults and children are referred to this hospital which is renowned for its achievements in this field. Long- or short-term, all the patients require a high degree of one-to-one nursing care and physiotherapy. The recovery process tends to be slow, patients need plenty of varied stimulus to regain speech, co-ordination, a degree of movement and possibly mobility.

Jackie, a sister, has worked in this unit for three years. She has been bringing her therapy dog, Simba, in to meet patients for some time.

'He started coming when he was a puppy, the patients so enjoyed seeing something so attractive and cuddly. As well as being young and enthusiastic, his personality and character made the patients smile. Even a smile is a breakthrough with some patients. A lack of ability to communicate or co-ordinate, a period of depression, or being in intermittent pain doesn't give you a lot to smile about! Adjusting to their injuries takes a long time for many patients. For the nursing staff, finding a response that is proactive is a major key to recovery.

"The dog is not a cure, but it can bring pleasure and a different stimulus into their daily routine. A dog can stimulate communication skills – the desire to attempt to say the dog's name or, for some, stringing a sentence together, to talk of previous experiences with a dog, are just two of the benefits the visiting dog can achieve. The dog can encourage movement, a turn of the head, eye movement, a smile or a hand or arm stretching out to touch or stroke. For some patients, these small skills have to be relearned and practised for an improvement in their condition to come about."

As Sylvia and Clyde move from patient to patient, it is evident from the instantaneous smiles that he is a very welcome visitor. This large dog is guided skilfully by Sylvia into the correct position next to a bed or chair, ensuring that they are not interfering with catheters, or, in the case of one patient with a tracheotomy, checking that the dust and hair from the dog are not going to cause problems. Clyde's tail gently wags as he is encouraged to jump up calmly and put his paws on the arms of a wheelchair.

The young boy is paralysed and is unable to bend his head forward, so the dog has to stand tall for the child to make eye contact. The smile that spread across his face said it all. The physiotherapist was delighted: eye movement and a smile are seen as positive progress. "You don't smile like that when you see me," she teased. The child's eyes flicked from the dog to the physiotherapist and he smiled at her, but his attention went straight back to the dog!

The staff are also very pleased to see the dogs. Apart from enjoying the positive reaction shown by their patients, they too enjoy a hug and a cuddle with the dog. As a nurse knelt on the floor and laid her head on the dog's back with her arms around Clyde's neck, she explained what she saw as some of the benefits of the visits. "For the nurses, it's a moment's respite from a demanding job! The dogs and their owners bring a change of conversation around the wards and the best tonic of all is when the dog does something at some point of the visit that makes you laugh."

Jackie stresses: "In this unit there is the need for the dog's visits to be monitored by a

Simba (left) and Clyde (right) are a well-known Golden double-act at Bath's Royal National Hospital.

trained nurse throughout. It's one job that no one minds doing. A therapy dog usually comes once a week. We have a rota of four different dogs that come and the owners fit in to our busy daily schedule. The nurse accompanying the visit is there to make sure the patients are content in the presence of the dog. **,**

The unit is looking at ways of introducing the dogs as an aid to the therapy work. The patients could be encouraged to do a variety of exercises involving the dog. Stretching out to touch, and pulling or throwing a toy for the dog are some of the ideas that are being considered at present. I am sure with the correct approach it could be very successful. Clyde certainly seems to be able to stimulate and motivate patients to try to participate.

Clyde's cheerful and gentle temperament has made him many friends in the ward.

CASE HISTORY

SUZANNE DIXON AND BARNEY

Name: Suzanne Dixon.
PAT Dog: Barney, a four-year-old
Bichon Frisé

Suzanne already had a therapy dog – Kass, a Staffordshire Bull Terrier, who visited a local psychiatric hospital – and decided that Barney's laid-back character and love of people would make him an ideal therapy dog, too.

' Most people think that therapy dogs just go into hospitals and homes for the elderly and disabled. Barney is an exceptional dog who does a different kind of work in a different type of environment.

"Barney began visiting Fell Dyke Primary School, where I work as a nursery nurse, when he was five-and-a-half months old, just to see what he would be like with all the hustle and bustle. He was brilliant with everyone,

especially the children, so I decided to apply for him to become a therapy dog. Barney had a temperament test, which he passed with flying colours.

"Barney goes to school on a weekly basis, every Thursday, unless he is needed elsewhere in the school (in which case he goes in when he is required). He is an excellent asset to our team and he is now part of the curriculum. The children take on the responsibilities of caring for a pet. They help to feed, walk, brush and bath him.

"They take their responsibilities very seriously. The school is situated on a very busy main road on the outskirts of a town. The children are very concerned just in case Barney gets out by accident and gets hurt, so they watch out for his well-being.

"Barney is highly thought of at Fell Dyke, so much so that we have made a 'Barney Wall'. On this wall is Barney's life-story, including details of his mother and father, Barney as a puppy, Barney at dog shows, and the children bathing him in the water-tray at school.

"Barney was in school during the week we

Barney is a big hit with these primary school pupils.

had an official inspection. The children had to make him a waterproof coat, and they also put reflective spots on it, just in case he went out in the dark. The inspectors were so impressed with him, that they wrote about him in the official report!

"Barney's typical day at school starts when he waits by the door through which the children enter the main building on a morning. Then he goes into the reception class (children aged four and five years) and waits for the children to get into a circle, so that he can get into the middle of them and have a stroke from all 28 members of the class. In the beginning, the children used to fight over who stroked him; now they don't mind as they know they all get to stroke him.

"During the day, Barney goes outside into the yard with all the children in the infant department, about 80-100 children. If Barney is out with the children and someone comments that he is a nice Poodle, the children get annoyed and say "He's not a Poodle, he's a Bichon Frisé!"; and when someone says that they have a "black one at home", the children reply "No, you can't have, because they only come in white."

"We have had some phobic children and

Barney's wall – where the children display their work about him.

parents who have been absolutely terrified of dogs, but, after a few weeks with Barney, they are fine. One pupil's mother had a bad experience with dogs when she was young and she had, as a result, transferred her feelings to the daughter, who was, in turn, frightened of dogs. After a few years of the daughter

The pupils are taught responsible pet care. Here they are learning how to bath and groom a dog.

attending the school and the mother visiting, these two are now the first to greet Barney every morning. They also buy him presents at Christmas and chocolate bones at Easter.

"Barney is a fabulous dog and affects so many people in his everyday life. He really is exceptional. **,**

WORKING THERAPY DOG

Once a dog has succeeded in being registered as a therapy dog, the owner will receive details of any visiting vacancies in their area. Any new institution that gives permission to visit must sign an acceptance form confirming that the therapy dog is welcome.

The name and address of the local co-ordinator is also provided. These experienced therapy dog owners have usually started to build a reputation locally, and can help to contact doctors, district nurses, social services or local hospitals.

Approaching these professionals can be daunting, but like most situations, if you don't ask you don't get! The more people ask about visiting with their therapy dogs, the more people get to know about the scheme and the easier it gets. Each local health authority is quite small and your fame, or, more accurately, your dog's fame, soon spreads!

There are so many people that do this work in the community, giving their time and sharing

Charlie adds some variety to the lives of the residents he visits.

their dog and life experiences with others. Unless you have been on the receiving end of this voluntary work you will probably be unaware that it goes on. Margaret Bramall with her therapy dog, a Golden Retriever called Charlie, explains: "I have spent time in hospital, and missed the attention that a dog can give. I feel I have experienced a little of what some patients or residents in homes for the elderly go through. There is nothing like the unconditional love a dog can offer. Plus I have made so many friends and go out and about far more because of my dog. A dog can boost the confidence of the shy, initiate conversation with passers-by, encourage you to join training classes and mix with other like-minded folk. They are a real tonic."

Therapy dog owners and co-ordinators are all volunteers and give their time and travelling expenses freely. It is a serious commitment – once a dog starts to visit on a weekly or monthly basis, the patients look forward to seeing him next time. For some, it is the only outside contact they have, other than with the staff. Great importance is placed on the dog's attendance by those that are visited. It is not a commitment to take on lightly: if you dissapoint patients, it can have a devastating effect.

Therapy dog Harriet is one of thousands of dogs who bring happiness to patients around the country.

CASE HISTORY

LEWIS TURNER AND ARNIE

Name: Lewis Turner.
PAT Dog: Arnie, Jack Russell Terrier.

Arnie is a broken-coated white and tan Jack Russell, who has a full tail and very short legs.

' We chose Arnie because he was friendly and was the first to run up to us when we viewed the litter. He was also the puppy that wriggled and made funny noises when we picked him up. Even at that age he was a dog with character.

"I wanted to get involved with PAT Dogs because my family and I received a lot of help and support from people who gave their time freely, after my brother died in a road accident. He was only twenty-six years old; I was twenty-four. It was a very difficult time for me and my family. I now feel I want to give *my* time and share my delightful dog with others. I have noticed that a lot of volunteers in this type of work are ex-patients or people who have suffered similarly.

"I thought Arnie might be suitable as a therapy dog when he was only four months old. Once I had overcome his stubborn nature (a continuous challenge), and when he had achieved a suitable level of obedience and understanding, my wife, Sarah, and I decided to set the application procedure in process.

"There were forms to fill in and agreements to sign, and, most importantly, Arnie had to be tested by an official recognised by the organisation. Both Sarah and I wanted to be accepted as therapy dog visitors so we both had to handle Arnie during his test. Arnie had to carry out basic obedience commands (Sit, Down, Stay, Heel and Come), firstly in a quiet situation and then in the company of other dogs. No sign of aggression must be shown.

"Arnie was put through his paces by Sandra Oliver, a qualified dog trainer from our local training club. Once she had recorded her opinions of the dog's response to control commands, she wanted to assess Arnie's general behaviour. She wanted to see how gently Arnie takes treats from us and from strangers. He is very polite – he takes them from your fingers and usually places them on the floor and inspects them. I am sure he

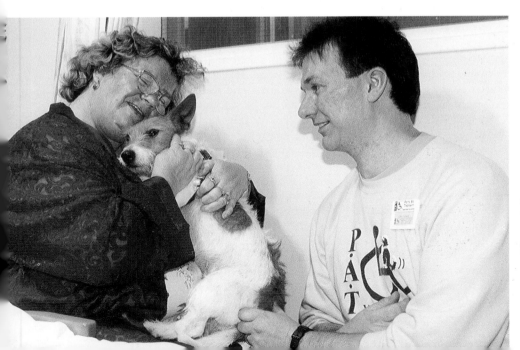

**Arnie is a little dog with a big personality, who just loves being loved.
Courtesy of Cambridge Newspapers.**

thinks we are trying to poison him. If the treat is tempting enough, he may deign to eat it!

"Another part of the test looks at how the dog reacts to different ways of being approached. Most dogs can cope with people approaching in a calm, quiet, unthreatening manner. Therapy dogs may have to cope with much worse. Arnie was tested by adults and children approaching him quickly, from behind, leaning over him and generally behaving in an erratic manner as they came up to him to fuss and praise him.

"Once we had passed our test, we approached Addenbrookes Hospital in Cambridgeshire to see if they were interested in a therapy dog visiting on a regular basis. We were all interviewed by Eileen Robertson, the Head of Voluntary Services based at the hospital. She needed to check that both dog and owners were suitable volunteers. They also discussed which wards would be suitable. To

be able to visit the children's wards, we had to have police clearance. Security at Addenbrookes, as with any hospital, is crucial – though it amused us that Arnie also had his photograph taken and was issued with an identity badge. His badge is still a great talking point – and icebreakers are useful.

"Visits can be difficult when you first start. The staff were not used to a PAT Dog visiting, and we had a lot of explaining to do. The nurses work shifts, so, for a while, it seemed every time we went, we had to start all over again. We always report to the ward nurses' station first. It is important to check if it is a good time, if there are patients to be avoided for one reason or another, and whether any have special needs. It takes a lot of nerve walking into a ward and saying, 'Hello, I'm Lewis and this is my dog, Arnie'. After a while, it becomes second nature.

"We probably do as much staff and patient

visitor therapy as we do patient therapy. One memorable example was when Arnie and I went into a ward where a lovely old lady was lying quietly in bed, looking at the ceiling, sad and depessed. Beside the bed sat her two daughters, also quiet and looking glum. Nobody was saying a word and the mood was heavy. I took a deep breath and introduced myself and Arnie. Mum sat up and exclaimed with joy how nice it was to see such a delightful little dog. Arnie, who seems to have sixth sense, hopped on to the bed (something the nurses turn a blind eye to), lay down beside her, snuggled in and went to sleep. All four of us chatted for a while.

"I eventually had to make my excuses and, after a last hug from Arnie, we moved on. When I looked back, both daughters were crying happy tears and Mum was still chatting. It gave me a terrific buzz. Getting a response like that is what makes visiting enjoyable for me.

"Another memorable visit came after we had been PAT Dog visiting for just three months. We came across an elderly blind lady who was bed-bound. I was told she was a dog lover and that she would enjoy meeting Arnie. I put Arnie on the bed. I've noticed Arnie's behaviour is different when he first meets a blind person. He lay beside the women totally still and completely relaxed, he stayed completely still while she ran her hands all over him. She exclaimed, 'What a lovely Jack Russell!'. In response, Arnie snuggled in tight and slept in her arms while we chatted. She was thrilled – we became instant friends and visited regularly. Arnie always behaves in the same way with blind people. He stays very still until given a signal to do otherwise. How he knows, I don't know!

"Arnie has also helped out in the rehabilitation unit. On one particular day, there were two dogs visiting at the same time, Arnie and Charlie. A young lady called Nicky was receiving treatment and physiotherapy for extensive injuries. To encourage her to exercise her hands and feet at the same time, Arnie lay on the bed beside Nicky where she managed to open her fingers and stroke and knead the dog's back and neck. At the same time, Charlie, a large Newfoundland, lay beside the bed, and Nicky was encouraged to stretch and touch Charlie with her feet and toes. She said it was the best physio session she had for a long time and much more enjoyable!

"For Arnie, the best visits are when we go to the children's ward. We are always accompanied by a nurse as we go around, to ensure the children are happy in the presence of the dog. From the minute we step through the door Arnie is on his toes and his tail never stops wagging. He literally prances around the ward. However, when there is a child to speak to, he is calm, relaxed and very careful. He is so good-tempered, even with the children who are a little rough. Some have unintentionally pulled his ears, tail or coat, but he takes it all in his stride.

"On a recent visit to a school, we were invited to give a talk on the work of PAT Dogs. They all wanted to touch Arnie, and he disappeared into a sea of children! All I could see was the lead being passed from child to child. Many other dogs would have been overwhelmed. Not Arnie – he reappeared from the excited mass, looking calm and collected. ,

CASE HISTORY

SANDRA OLIVER AND CHARLIE

Name: Sandra Oliver.
PAT Dog: Charlie, a Newfoundland.

Charlie is a two-year-old Newfoundland, weighing in at 12 stone. His owner tells me he still has some growing to do! This gentle giant belongs to Sandra Oliver, a professional dog trainer who took Charlie when he was four-and-half months old.

Sandra with Charlie, a big dog with a big heart.

'Right from getting Charlie, I had decided to train him as a prospective therapy dog. I had listened to a talk by a therapy dog owner during my course to become a qualified dog training instructor. I was so impressed with the effect that a dog could have on a long-stay patient, a person living in a residential home for the elderly, or a nursing home, that I decided this was an excellent way to channel my dog-training ability and interest.

"It was important during early training to distinguish between the calm, quiet approach required for therapy dog training and the enthusiasm required for obedience training. I started by using a different lead and collar for the different training sessions. Newfoundlands are brighter than a lot of people think; Charlie was quick to cotton on.

"I taught him to approach people calmly and sit in front of them to be touched and praised. He learned to sit close to wheelchairs and beds so people were able to reach him. He had to be conditioned to ignore sudden noises and erratic movement. My calm approach and attitude in these situations helped to develop Charlie's personality and the desired behaviour of a good therapy dog.

"He passed his test. I knew he would not let me down, but as co-ordinator and trainer at the local dog-training classes, I did feel under pressure. I was delighted to get my official clearance and start visiting. I was very lucky when I started with my visits, as I had the support of Lewis and Arnie (page 92) who were old hands at it! This helped me through my initial lack of confidence with first introductions to patients and approaches to new hospitals and homes.

"As an area co-ordinator for Pets As Therapy, I get to meet all sorts of people and many different types of dog. One of my responsibilities is to carry out the assessment of prospective therapy dogs. I like the owner to bring their dog along to be tested at the training classes. This gives me an opportunity to see the dog on unfamiliar ground in the company of other dogs and with plenty of other people available to help with the assessment. I enjoy doing the testing; you get to meet some lovely dogs and make new friends with the owners.

"One of our weekly visits is to Addenbrookes Hospital. Charlie and I both had to get clearance from the voluntary

Despite his size, patients who are otherwise nervous of dogs are able to interact with this gentle giant. Courtesy of Kent Newspapers

services officer and the police to be able to visit the children's ward. With our identity card attached, we visit 11 wards, which can sometimes take up to three hours. The bright eyes and smiles make it all worthwhile.

"Charlie and I regularly visit the stroke ward. One patient, an elderly gentleman, was surrounded by family when we arrived on the ward. The relatives asked if Charlie could come and sit beside the gentleman. His bed was lowered by the nurse and she then took his hand and moved it through Charlie's coat. Since the stroke, his hand had been tightly clenched, but slowly it started to uncurl. Visiting this gentleman became a regular stop on our rounds and he slowly progressed to gently feeling and rubbing Charlie's coat. Arriving some weeks later, it gave me great pleasure to see him holding his granddaughter's hand, and it wasn't long before the gentleman was able to go home.

"Sometimes you can get a reaction that is a bit unexpected. Yvonne, another patient on the stroke ward, burst into floods of tears the first time she saw Charlie. She buried her head into Charlie's neck and sobbed inconsolably. When she let go, we quietly moved on as I was concerned that I was distressing her. The following week, we had the same reaction. As each week passed, the tears got less and eventually Yvonne was able to explain why she cried when she saw Charlie. Sadly, she had to rehome her three-year-old Golden Retriever and missed the dog so much. The three of us enjoyed our weekly visits. A real bond developed and we all cried the day Yvonne was well enough to return home!

"With children and adults, Charlie's behaviour is exceptional. We experience a variety of situations and emotions. Patients who are reluctant to talk to others will often talk to me and Charlie. Patients or residents that have never touched a dog before will feel confident to stroke Charlie. The chatter and buzz we seem to create in a previously quiet ward or day room is marvellous and Charlie offers a change of subject and attitude to the usual bedside conversation. These are just some of the reasons why I enjoy visiting – it is so fulfilling! Sharing my generous dog, who readily gives his love and attention to all who need it, gives me so much pleasure. **,**